Embracing the Love of God

Other books by James Bryan Smith

A Spiritual Formation Workbook

Devotional Classics
(editor with Richard J. Foster)

EMBRACING THE LOVE OF GOD

The Path and Promise of Christian Life

JAMES BRYAN SMITH

HarperOne
An Imprint of HarperCollinsPublishers

For information about Renovaré,
write to Renovaré, 8 Inverness Drive East
Suite 102, Enlgewood, CO 80112
or log on to the Web site: http//www.renovaré.org

HarperCollins Web site: http://www.harpercollins.com

HarperCollins®, ■®, and HarperOne™ are trademarks of
HarperCollins Publishers.

Library of Congress Cataloging-in-Publication Data
is available upon request.

ISBN 978-0-06-154269-5

23 24 25 26 27 LBC 19 18 17 16 15

To Meghan and Jacob
my beloved wife and precious son

The only thing that matters
is faith working through love.

GALATIANS 5:16

Contents

Acknowledgments

The community of people to which I am indebted is too large to be named, but there are certain people whose contributions I would like to recognize. First, I am grateful for the friendship and encouragement of Richard J. Foster, whose belief in me made this book possible. I owe much to Brennan Manning, whose life and writings and friendship inspired me to enter the path of embracing God's love.

I am extremely indebted to Kandace Hawkinson, whose editorial skills continually amazed me, and whose firm belief in this project made it possible. I would also like to thank Jennifer Jantz, Patrick Sehl, Catherine Clarke, Jeremy Davis, and Penny and Emil Johnson, whose careful reading and insightful comments helped shape the writing of this book. In addition, I am also grateful for the friendship and wisdom of

Rich Mullins, the consistent belief and support of Mike Smith and Vicki and Scott Price, the pastoral guidance of Jeff Gannon, and the heartfelt encouragement of David Castleberry. In addition, I would like to thank the administration of Friends University, particularly Biff Green and Bob Dove, who allowed me the time I needed to write this book.

I would also like to thank my mother and father, Calvin and Wanda Smith, who raised me in a home full of acceptance, forgiveness, and care, providing living examples of God's love that are etched into my memory. Finally, I want to say how blessed I am to have such a wonderful wife, Meghan, who never stopped believing in the importance of this book, and who was willing to make many sacrifices so that I could write it.

Foreword

The most wonderful thing that can happen to any human being is to be loved. It alone speaks to the gnawing sense of insignificance and isolation we feel. And the marvelous news is that we have been loved and we are loved, each and every one of us. Uniquely and individually. At the heart of the universe is love, divine love, personal, intimate God-love for you and for me. We are known! We are chosen! We are loved! Once experienced at the deepest levels of the soul, no reality can be more profoundly disturbing, more radically healing, more utterly transforming.

James Bryan Smith speaks passionately of this "furious love of God." In a hundred different ways he whispers to us: "You are loved!" "You are accepted!" "You are under the forgiving mercy and tender care of God!"

The structure of this book is deceptively simple: Under the overarching love of God we receive God's acceptance of us so we can accept ourselves and others; we welcome God's forgiveness of us so we can forgive ourselves and others; we embrace God's care for us so we can care for ourselves and others. But do not allow this simplicity to lead you into thinking that these ideas are simplistic. Nothing can touch us more profoundly than the experience of God's loving heart. Reporters once asked the great theologian Karl Barth, "What is the most profound thought you have ever had?" His reply: "Jesus loves me this I know, for the Bible tells me so."

And so it is. If I know, really know, that God loves me, everything is changed. I am no longer a trifling speck in a meaningless cosmos. I am an eternal creature of infinite worth living in a universe animated by love and care and friendship.

We find this reality so hard to believe because it is an invisible reality, and everything and everyone has trained us to view as real only what we can see, touch, and kick . . . and get kicked by.

And yet eternity is in our hearts. Maybe, just maybe, our universe is populated in ways we can hardly imagine. Maybe what we call empty space is not empty at all but teeming with life and love and God's animating presence throughout. Maybe, just maybe, behind all things is real intelligence: intelligence that is wholly personal; intelligence that is wholly other than us but that also has freely chosen to be involved in the affairs of this universe—and, in fact, at one pinpoint in human history, did indeed become so intimately involved as to be incarnated as a baby, a baby who grew to be a man and lived like no one ever lived and died like no one ever died. All so that we could see love with skin on it. And then this man rose from the dead so we could know that this One who is Love lives on eternally, and that we can participate in his life, loving and being loved, now and forever.

Certainly this is the picture the Bible gives us about our existence. And yet we can hardly believe it. If only it were true. . . . Dear God, could it be true? *Embracing the Love of God* helps us in our search for the answer.

Richard J. Foster

Introduction

*And we are put on this earth a little space
that we may learn to bear the beams of love.*

WILLIAM BLAKE

It was 4:00 A.M. and my six-month-old son was crying. It was time for his bottle and it was my turn to feed him. I went into the nursery, picked him up, cradled him in my arms, and gave him his bottle, which quickly calmed him down. As he lay in my lap, he looked up at me and smiled. Our eyes were fixed on one another. I welled up with a warm feeling of love.

"I love you, Jacob," I said spontaneously. "I only wish I could communicate that to you. *I hope some day you will understand how much I love you.*"

Then it occurred to me: he *already* knows he is loved. Though he doesn't have the words to describe it or explain it, he *feels* it. Love is in the room, in my hands and arms as I hold him, in my words as I soothe him. It is written on my face. It is in my eyes. The same is true between God and ourselves. God said to Moses,

> "Speak to Aaron and his sons, saying, 'Thus you shall bless the Israelites: You shall say to them, The LORD bless you and keep you; *the LORD make his face to shine upon you,* and be gracious to you; *the LORD* lift up his countenance upon you, and give you peace'" (Num. 6:23–26).[1]

God is essentially telling his people: "When I look at you I smile, and I want you to know that."

I have come to believe that God is madly in love with us. God loves us with a passionate love. It is too great for us to comprehend; we do not have the words to describe it fully. It is too vast to grasp completely. *But we can know it. And we can feel it.* It is in his hands as he holds us. It is in his gentle words as he comforts us. It is written all over his face.

And yet, many of us feel alienated from God. We are a technologically advanced society, but our souls are sick. We seek help in psychotherapy, support groups, tarot cards, crystals—anything that will relieve the pain. But we find that these supposed sources of help are helpless. The emptiness will not be filled.

"We've had a hundred years of psychotherapy—and the world's getting worse," says James Hillman, a past president of the American Psychiatric Association.[2] Tinkering with the psyche, searching through our past, and examining our behavior may provide personal illumination, but they do not ease our alienated soul.

A man in a psychiatrist's office was overheard saying, "Make me sure that there is a God of love and I shall go away a well man."[3] His cry is the cry of all of us: make us sure there is a God of love. It is what we desire most, even if we do not have the words to express it.

One of the most difficult Christian doctrines to believe is the incredible value of human beings. It is difficult for many of us to accept God's love, to believe that God looks upon us and smiles. It is hard, noted William Blake, to bear the beams of God's love. We must *learn* to bear them. What we long to know is that we are loved. To be more specific, we hunger to know that we are accepted as we are, forgiven for all we have done, and cared for by a gracious, loving God. When we know this we walk away well.

God's love comes down to us, fills our hearts, and is then extended to our neighbor. When we know and feel and experience God's love we cannot *but* love ourselves. This kind of self-love is nothing like the cheap form of narcissism peddled in our culture. It is a genuine, comprehensive kind of love that is based not on what we do but on who we are.

When this love begins to penetrate our hearts, it will naturally flow out to those around us. Loving one another will be less difficult and more natural. When we realize we have been accepted as we are, we are enabled to accept others as they are. When we grasp that we have been forgiven for all that we have done, we find that we are empowered to forgive others for what they have done. When we comprehend that we are valued and cared for by God, we are provided the means to value and care for others.

When Jesus was asked to sum up the whole of the Law, he answered by coupling the great Deuteronomy edict about loving God (6:4) and the seemingly lesser law of Leviticus about loving your neighbor (19:8): "You shall love the Lord your God with all your heart, and with all your soul, and with all your strength, and with all your mind; *and* your neighbor as yourself" (Luke 10:27).

Why did Jesus combine them? Because he knew that they were essentially one law. Love comes from one source: God. We love, said John, because God first loved us (1 John 4:19). In the face of God's magnificent love for us, we cannot but love in return.

When that love is known and felt by us, it affects how we view ourselves and, ultimately, how we view one another. God's love for us results in a proper love for ourselves, and then extends to love for our neighbors. Paul, like Jesus, summed up the whole of the Christian life when he said, *"the only thing that matters is faith working through love"* (Gal. 5:6).

A few years ago I realized that I did not love God with all that I am, nor did I love my neighbor, nor even myself. I asked God to begin teaching me, and since then I have been on a journey of love. God has exposed me to many people, books, and events that drive home the same point: You are loved. This book is a result of that journey. It is written so that you might be able to hear God's gentle voice calling to you, "I love you. I love you. I love you."

Loving is not difficult. *Knowing* we are loved is. Learning to live in the reckless confidence that God loves us is a process. Each day I continue to learn more and more about the depth of God's devotion. Life is a journey, not a destination. We never arrive. And yet the path along which we walk is marked by certain promises. These promises are fixed, solid, and secure;

they are stable, bound, and firmly fastened for all eternity, even if we do not trust in them. God whispers them into our soul: "I love you. I am with you always—no matter what you have done. You are precious to me. I will never leave you."

These promises are, I believe, the foundational beliefs of the Christian faith. They are the truths that inspired men and women such as St. Paul, St. Augustine, Martin Luther, Evelyn Underhill, Bernard of Clairvaux, Julian of Norwich, John Wesley, and Thomas Merton—people whose voices echo throughout this book. I hope that the ideas put forth are not so much mine as they are the basic beliefs of the Church. They are, at the very least, the doctrines that have shaped my spiritual life. As the English author G. K. Chesterton said of the Christian faith, "I did not make it. God and humanity made it; and *it made me*."[4]

This book is for people who, like me, desire to hear that whisper, for those of us who long to let God take the pain in our lives and make us whole. In short, this book is for anyone who yearns to be embraced by the love of God. My prayer for you as you read is the same prayer St. Paul once prayed for the Christians in Ephesus:

> I pray that you may have the power to comprehend, with all the saints, what is the breadth and length and height and depth, and *to know the love of Christ* that surpasses knowledge, so that you may be filled with all the fullness of God (Eph. 3:18–19).

PART ONE

KNOWING GOD'S ACCEPTANCE

Chapter 1

GOD'S ACCEPTANCE

By loving us, God makes us lovable.

<small>ST. AUGUSTINE</small>

One morning, long after becoming a Christian, I woke to the realization that I was avoiding God.

I had been trying so very hard for a very long time to be the kind of person I thought God wanted me to be, but I had failed, over and over, to be that person. I was sure that God was ashamed of me, of my weaknesses, cowardice, and pride. I knew that I was ashamed of myself.

I could barely stand to look in the mirror. The person I saw in the reflection was flawed, imperfect, and had fallen short of God's expectations and my own. I felt that I deserved judgment. So I stayed away from solitude and prayer and instead kept myself busy, hoping to overcome my feeling of failure through good works.

But on this day I decided to face God again. I knelt down and confessed all of my sins and weaknesses, and I begged God to take away my flaws. I told God I would do better, try harder, and that I was sorry for having failed so many times.

I had done this before, of course. And even though I was making a thorough and heartfelt confession, I still felt alienated from God. The silence was deafening. I felt all alone. In my nervousness I found myself chattering away at God: "I am so sorry, please forgive me, I know I can do better . . ."

Then suddenly, the Spirit spoke within me: "Be quiet, Jim, and close your eyes."

When I closed my eyes I saw a lush green field, with the wind blowing through the high grass. Jesus was standing off in the distance and he began walking toward me. As he got closer I began pleading once again, "I am so sorry, please forgive me, I know I can do better . . ."

Jesus never said a word in response. He just kept walking toward me, looking straight into my eyes. When he got near me he lifted me up from the ground and hugged me. For the next five minutes I was hugged by God. No words were spoken, but a feeling of warmth and love and acceptance penetrated my lonely, restless heart.

Sinners in the Hands of an Angry God

The above experience occurred eight years after I became a Christian. Though my life with God did not begin in this place, my life was changed by this. I had expected and feared God's disappointment, but I was shown God's love. Today I cannot say that the struggle to feel God's complete and utter acceptance is over, but I can say that my sense of alienation has been largely replaced by a sense of union.

From where did my feelings of alienation come? They did not appear overnight, but instead were the result of many years of being exposed to messages of condemnation and guilt. No one had ever fully explained to me the core concept of the Christian faith, the message that God loves us, searches after us, and longs for us to be whole. I heard bits and pieces of this gospel, but never enough to fill my heart. In its absence I created my own theology, a patchwork quilt made up of false images of God.

As a consequence, I lived my early Christian life with the belief that God really did not like me. God tolerated me, I thought, in the hopes of improving me. One day I just might get myself together, quit sinning, and start behaving like Jesus. Then, I was certain, God would approve of me.

I got up early almost every day, praying and reading the Bible between five and seven in the morning. I fasted once a week, spent time helping the poor, and maintained straight A's in all of my classes. I entertained the idea of becoming a monk because I figured that by abandoning the pleasures of this world I would please God even more.

In a slow, almost imperceptible way, I developed an unhealthy conception of God. As a result, the Christian life became a painful drudgery. On the outside I appeared joyful and upbeat, but beneath the holy veneer lurked a bitter and unhappy person who secretly hated himself and the god he served.

The God We Make in Our Image

Many of us find it difficult to believe that God could look at us and smile. For years I viewed God as a judge, as do most of the people I know. The god I served was angry with me, ready to punish me for a slight infraction. I never knew where I stood with this god. If I lived flawlessly, I might, for a few moments, feel secure, but for the most part I did not. Much of the problem was that I viewed God as a person much like myself. I created this god in my own image. Like me, this god was capable of love, but it was a conditional love. This god was mostly cold and distant, exact with his judgment and severe with his punishment.

This god of my religious imagination was eventually replaced by the real God, the God of Abraham, the Father of Jesus. But the change did not occur overnight. The false idol I had created had to be slowly melted down by the fire of God's furious love.

Christian author Peter van Breeman writes, "If we think God is a person who can divide his love, then we are thinking not of God but ourselves. God is perfectly one, the perfect unity. We *have* love, but God *is* love. His love is not an activity. It is his whole self."[1]

God does not love, God *is* love (1 John 4:16). I am capable of loving, but I am also capable of not loving. That cannot be said about God. God cannot stop loving, because love is God's nature. It is not my nature to love. I must learn to love, and only by God's grace am I able to love as he loves.

God Loves First and Always

The verse that began a change in my thinking about God was 1 John 4:10: "For herein is love, not that we love God, but that God first loved us by sending his Son as a sacrifice for our sins." As I meditated on these words it occurred to me that God loved me long before I ever loved him in return.

Even when I was far and distant from God, God loved me first. Even when I was unbelieving and angry with God, God loved me first. Even when I was serving a false god, God loved me first. This began to permeate my whole attitude toward God. It was the first stage of understanding God's acceptance of me.

One day I stumbled upon a prayer written by Søren Kierkegaard that shed light on the true nature of God and his love:

> You have loved us first, O God, alas! We speak of it in terms of history as if You loved us first but a single time, rather than that without ceasing You have loved us first many times and everyday and our whole life through. When we wake up in the morning and turn our soul toward You—You are there first—You have loved us first; if I rise at dawn and at that same second turn my soul toward You in prayer, You are there ahead of me, You have loved me first. When I withdraw from the distractions of the day and turn my soul toward You, You are there first and thus forever. And we speak ungratefully as if You have loved us first only once.[2]

I had understood God's love as something historical, something that had happened once, but Kierkegaard's prayer taught me that God's love is constant, ever-present, and un-changing. Every moment of every day God is with me, loving me first.

For me, the initial step in coming to understand God's acceptance was an intellectual one. The truth of God's love was formed in my mind as I read and reflected on the Bible, but it will take a long time for these truths to sink down into my heart completely. All along my path I encounter these radi-cal promises of God's love, and I let each one penetrate my thoughts and flow into my feelings. God's love slowly be-comes my reality.

Everything Is Enwrapped in Love

In addition to the promises of the Bible, I found that the world is filled with signs of God's love and acceptance. All around us are hints and evidences of God's desire for us to be full of joy. These signs show us that God's love surpasses what we can know. If we look at them closely and meditate on their good-ness, we will find ourselves crying out, "You really love me, don't you God?"

The first sign is creation itself. We live in a world that is magnificent and beyond our understanding. In the created world around us, wrote the great devotional teacher Evelyn Underhill, "we see the Eternal Artist, Eternal Love at work."[3]

For many years I did not have the eyes to see the glory of creation. I was trained to see the world from a scientific per-spective. Nature was never majestic; it was just a hunk of mat-ter and molecules spinning endlessly in a pattern of evolution.

But a single statement by G. K. Chesterton changed the way I look at the world around me. He pointed out that nature is not a system of necessity. Yes, the sun will probably come up tomorrow, but it need not. Perhaps each day God says to the sun, "Arise! Go forth!" Yes, grass is typically green, but it need not be. God could make it purple if he wished.

There are no "laws" of nature. God can do whatever he wishes. Frogs jump and birds fly and water runs down hill not because of "laws" but because, writes Chesterton, God wishes them to do so. He notes, "It is not a necessity, for though we can count on it practically, we have no right to say that it must always happen."[4]

I remember walking out in my backyard after reading those words, looking at the grass and the trees and the birds, and thinking, "Wow!" That is the only word I said for several minutes. The air, the morning light, the leaves that shook in the wind, looked, well . . . like magic. Instead of seeing them as some kind of dead prop in the drama of my life, I saw them as wondrous gifts spoken forth from the mouth of God.

"Look at the grass . . . it's, it's green," I said like a fool in complete wonder. I think I saw the grass, really saw it, for the first time. It was declaring its Maker's praise. It was green and soft by divine decree. And suddenly I was rolling in it like a dog, with my legs in the air, laughing out loud and not caring if the neighbors saw me. The mystery of creation moved me to joy. I knew I was loved. I knew what the fourteenth-century mystic Julian of Norwich meant when she wrote, "Everything is enwrapped in love and is part of a world produced not by mechanical necessity but by a passionate desire."[5]

A Love Affair

"Christianity," writes contemporary author and speaker Brennan Manning, "is not essentially a philosophy of love but a love affair."[6] God's love for us is not a cold theory or a textbook formula. It is a living, passionate, searching love. Christianity is a love story. The Bible is a divine love letter from One who is forever reaching out to his people.

Too often we try to control God by defining his behavior. I attempted to tame God by reducing him to doctrines of grace and theories about salvation. My theology eventually failed. Tennyson once observed: "Our little systems have their day; they have their day and cease to be: they are but broken lights of thee, and thou, O Lord, art more than they."[7] My little system, my personal theology, was merely a "broken light" of the reality of God.

Philosophy tries to reduce God to a *first mover* and science attempts to remove God entirely. But God looms quietly in the wings and allows us such silly speculation. Contemporary author Frederick Buechner once noted that our attempts at *theology* are akin to a dung beetle looking up at a human and trying to do *humanology*.[8] Whatever we are allowed to discover about God, he is more.

When God revealed himself to me it blew my belief system to bits. Like Thomas Aquinas, I knew that all of my speculation was like straw compared to the reality of God. And like the lover in the Song of Solomon I could only respond, "Draw me after you" (Song of Sol. 1:4). God woos us like a lover who seeks his beloved. The torrid passion sometimes felt between two human beings is a pale reflection of the burning desire

God has for us. It was love, not a theory of redemption, that made the martyrs sing praise while being tortured. It was love, not a doctrine of the atonement, that kept Jesus on the cross.

God Proves His Love for Us

When he was a young boy, twelfth-century church leader Bernard of Clairvaux fell asleep outside a church while waiting to go in for a Christmas Eve service. In his sleep he had a dream, a kind of vision, in which he saw very clearly and distinctly how the Son of God, having espoused human nature, became a little child in his mother's womb. In that act he came to see how God's heavenly majesty was mingled with sweet humility. This vision so filled young Bernard's heart with comfort and jubilation that throughout his life he kept a vivid memory of it.[9]

What was it that filled his heart with joy? It was nothing other than the fact that God chose to be with us: Immanuel. Out of love Jesus was conceived, and out of love he chose to die. There is something in us that God finds lovable. It is certainly not our sanctity, nor is it our fidelity. When I look at my own baseness, my incredible ability to sin at a moment's notice, I wonder what God sees in me.

Just recently I experienced a wonderful hour of prayer. I felt all warm inside, centered on God's love, and ready to share that love with everyone I met. While driving to work a person cut me off on the freeway, and immediately I began screaming at him. Where did this anger come from? It was in me all along. It is a good thing that God does not wait for us to become perfect in order to accept us.

"But God proves his love for us in that while we still were sinners Christ died for us" (Rom. 5:8). God's love for us is amazing in that he loves us without much of a reason. If we doubt it, all we have to do is consider the birth, life, death, and resurrection of Christ. For centuries that has been the clearest sign of God's radical acceptance. Too often we reduce the cross to a mere decoration when in fact it is the most glorious demonstration of love that has ever been.

In Jesus we hear God saying to us, "What you cannot do for yourself, I myself will do. Your sin stands between us, and you cannot remove it, so I will do it for you. My blood will cleanse your sins, and I will remember them no more. Nothing will stand between us. I will rise from the dead so that you can live. My love is too strong for death to conquer. Once alive, I will invite you to die and rise with me. Eternal life is now available. It is in my Son."

Nothing Can Separate Us

For most of my Christian life I related to God on the basis of what I did for him. If I prayed well, studied hard, served much, and sinned little, then I felt reasonably sure God was pleased with me. I was living in a kind of fear that was paralyzing my ability to love God, love myself, and ultimately, love others. I was afraid that God would look at my faults and withdraw his love.

I was afraid that my weaknesses would separate me from the love of Christ. Now I see that they cannot. I was afraid that my sinfulness would separate me from the love of Christ. Now

I am certain that nothing will ever separate me from the love God has made visible in Jesus.

I see now how foolish it was to think that my feeble attempts at righteousness had anything to do with how God feels about me. For too long I was impressed with my "commitment" to Christ; now I am only impressed with Christ's commitment to me. My previous focus had been on my "decision" for Jesus; now I am concentrating on his decision for me.

By shifting the focus away from myself and onto Christ and his love for me, I have noticed that everything comes into view. When Martin Luther was suffering under the weight of guilt, his spiritual director, Johannes Staupitz, said, "Martin, quit looking at your sin and start looking at Jesus."[10] When Luther turned his eyes to Christ, the reformation of his spiritual life began. The effects of that shift were farther reaching than he ever could have imagined.

Nothing, absolutely nothing, can separate us from God's love. St. Paul reminded the Romans of this when he wrote, "For I am convinced that neither death, nor life, nor angels, nor rulers, nor things present, nor things to come, nor powers, nor height, nor depth, nor anything else in all creation, will be able to separate us from the love of God in Christ Jesus our Lord" (Rom. 8:38–39). God's love for us cannot be changed. Why? Because it is not based on anything we do.

It was the poet Gerard Manley Hopkins who declared, "I say that we are wound with mercy round and round—as with air."[11] We cannot escape God's love and mercy because it is everywhere. It enwraps and enfolds us wherever we go; it surrounds us and penetrates us even if we are not aware of it.

You Are Accepted

My pride led me to want to earn God's acceptance because I felt so unacceptable. My religious activities kept me from having to face my inner pain. By spending long hours at the church, taking on too many people's problems, and engaging in strenuous devotional exercises, I was longing to hear God say, "Well done."

Little by little I was able to open up to God—fearfully at first but with greater boldness as each time I was received with gentleness. I could come out of hiding because I felt accepted. It was absurd to think I could hide from God in the first place, but I tried nonetheless.

One of the hardest steps for me was to admit my weaknesses and failures. I had tried to cover them up, excuse them, and rationalize them. But each time I found myself baring my soul to God, I received not judgment but mercy.

God's love for me has radically reshaped my identity. I no longer need to defend myself, make resolutions to do better, or show God that I have atoned for my sins. God is slowly making me bold.

During the period in which I felt so alienated from God, I prayed, "Lord, why did you call me into ministry. I am not worthy. If the people I minister to knew all of my sins and shortcomings, they would not listen. I am not up to this." God's voice seemed to remind me, "Jim, I have never used anyone *but* sinners to share my good news, and I have never had it preached to anyone but sinners. The message is not about you, it is about me."

God loves me just as I am, not as I should be.[12] I know that I am not *as I should be*. I know there is a lot of sin that still needs to be rooted out of me. I know that God is not finished with me yet. But I know that I am loved. Modern writer Donald McCullough noted, "We may have more failures than achievements, we may not be wealthy or powerful, we may not even be happy, but we are nonetheless accepted by God, held in his hands. Such is the promise to us in Jesus Christ, a promise we can trust."[13]

We Did Not Earn It, We Cannot Lose It

We can trust in this promise because the promise is not based on anything we have done or will do. We do not deserve God's acceptance and love; it is a gift. Gifts have nothing to do with the merit of the receiver. If I work for something, I do not receive a gift, I receive my rightful wages. When we give a gift we are saying, "You did not earn this, and I do not owe you this, but I want to give it to you because I love you."

For years I related to God as if he sat in a swivel chair. When I did something good, God would look at me and smile. When I did something bad, God would turn his back to me until I made amends, when he would swivel back and accept me again. I kept God constantly on the move.

I thought of God's acceptance as something I could lose by my behavior. It was not logical for me to think this, since I did not do anything to gain God's acceptance in the first place. How can we lose something that we did not earn? If God loved us when we were estranged from him, how can we lose his love now that we have chosen to live in peace with him?

The Holy Spirit: The Outpouring of Love

God's love and acceptance of us is constant and never changes. How do we come to know of this love? The Holy Spirit is the agent that makes it known to us. Paul writes, "God's love has been poured into our hearts through the Holy Spirit that has been given to us" (Rom. 5:5). The Holy Spirit of God enters into us and whispers his love. Flesh and blood, logic and reason, will never reveal God's love to us. It is beyond our understanding; it must be revealed.

"The outpouring of the Holy Spirit is really the outpouring of his love," wrote French monk Abbé de Tourville.[14] The Holy Spirit is the continuation of the love of God seen in Jesus. The love between the Father and the Son is communicated to us through the Holy Spirit. We are temples in whom the Spirit of God dwells (1 Cor. 3:16; 6:19). God is love; love itself dwells within us. That is why John said we know we are born of God when we are able to love (1 John 3:14).

It is the voice of the Spirit within us that reminds us that we are the Beloved. If we listen closely, we will hear these words of love. They sound something like this:

> I have called you by name, from the very beginning. You are mine and I am yours. You are my Beloved, on you my favor rests. I have molded you from the depths of the earth and knitted you together in your mother's womb. I have carved you in the palms of my hands and hidden you in the shadow of my embrace. Has it crossed your

mind that I am proud you have accepted the gift of faith I have offered you? Proud that you have freely chosen me, after I had chosen you, as your friend and Lord? Proud that with all your warts and wrinkles you haven't given up? I never expected that you would be perfect.

I love you. I love you. I love you. Nothing will ever change that.[15]

Pray to Be Drawn

How do we come to know such love? We must ask for it. We must pray that we will come to know and feel this love. We must plead to God before we will hear this gentle voice. God will not delay in reply. But he is so gracious that he will never intrude. God has promised that if we seek him with all of our heart, we will find him: "When you search for me, you will find me; if you seek me with all your heart" (Jer. 29:13).

Frederick Buechner writes, "If you have never known the power of God's love, then maybe it is because you have never asked to know it—I mean really asked, expecting an answer."[16] Are you ready to ask? God is ready to give. Nothing gives God more pleasure than filling his children with love and hearing them exclaim, "Abba, Daddy!" (Rom. 8:14; Gal. 4:6).

Julian of Norwich once wrote, "The greatest honor we can give to Almighty God is to live gladly because of the knowledge of his love."[17] Ask God to give you this knowledge, not in your head but in your heart. Pray the prayer of eighteenth-century Italian saint Alphonsus Liguori until it becomes yours: "Dearest Lord, let your holy love possess me wholly."[18]

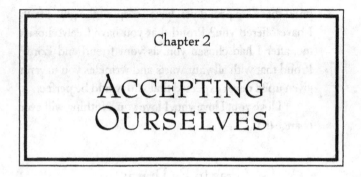

Chapter 2

ACCEPTING OURSELVES

What I am before God, that I am.

ST. FRANCIS OF ASSISI

The first day I met her she was wearing beach clothes. She carried a skateboard, and her hair looked wind-blown and wild. She was new to the college, and being a Christian, she wanted to meet the chaplain.

"You know, dude, like, Jesus is so totally awesome!" Sandy said. I did not speak much *surfer-ese*, but I got the gist of it. She bounced in her chair and smiled with reckless abandon. When she left the office I felt as if a storm had just blown through.

Sandy continued to come and visit and soon became a part of our weekly fellowship group. Her personality was often overbearing, but like a comic strip character, she was amusing and well liked. She made us laugh with her outrageous behavior and encouraged us with her positive attitude.

As our friendship grew she shared more and more of herself, her past, and her anxieties. During one of our discussions I noticed a change. It was so subtle I almost missed it. Right in the middle of a sentence Sandy's voice changed from her perky, upbeat tone to a more natural sound. Her words changed as well. No longer using surfer jargon, she spoke with a normal vocabulary. It was as if a new person had just entered the room. She left before I could make mention of it.

A few days later I saw her again. "Sandy, can I ask you about something?" I inquired.

"Sure, dude, like, yeah," she answered.

"The other day you seemed to change during our discussion for just a brief moment. This may not be my place to ask, but it made me wonder if the whole cheerleader-surfer persona is really you, or just someone you invented."

Her smile disappeared. "It is a character I invented," she said quietly. "I had to. I hated who I was inside, and I was afraid people would reject me." She told me how she had been badly abused by a relative, tossed from place to place, and told repeatedly how ugly and unlovable she was in words too dark and sinister to be repeated.

She created a character, she thought, as a defense, because if people still rejected her, it wouldn't be *her* they were rejecting, but the character. "If I let people see the real me they might reject me, and then, where would I be? The real me is all I have, and if they reject that, I have nowhere to go."

The Root of the Problem

In some small way, each and every day, most of us do just what Sandy did. We are uncertain as to whether or not we will be accepted, so we put on a mask or play a role we think others will like. At the root of the problem we fear rejection.

Best-selling author John Powell notes, "None of us wants to be a fraud or to live a lie; none of us wants to be a sham, a phony, but the fears that we experience and the risks that honest self-communication would involve seem so intense to us that seeking refuge in our roles, masks, and games becomes an almost natural reflex action."[1]

We all receive messages of condemnation from time to time. Teachers, parents, friends, and other significant people in our lives may tell us that we are "dumb" or "fat" or "not good enough." This forces us to find ways to protect ourselves. Sandy found safety in her character. During the next three years I watched the character fade away and the real Sandy emerge.

How did she grow? She discovered her true identity from God's perspective. Each week in our campus fellowship meetings we discussed the importance of seeing ourselves as God sees us. One evening we had a discussion about our sense of identity, discovering together that we are not what we do (which is constantly in flux), but rather, we are who God says we are.

Sandy began to settle into this notion. It was becoming clear to her that her past, her behavior, and her hurt did not determine her identity. Instead, she began to let her identity as a child of God, as one who is loved and accepted unconditionally, shape her behavior. She began to share her difficult past with others in the group. Seeing her received with acceptance and not condemnation, the rest of us were able to relax about ourselves and feel accepted by others. In the midst of a community of acceptance Sandy was able to establish a solid identity.

Trying to think well of herself or convincing others she was valuable was not the solution. The answer to her problem came in the discovery of God's acceptance of her, just as she was. All that remained was for her to accept herself, her true self, as God accepted her. In many ways, this is the hardest step.

Peter van Breeman observes, "It is fairly easy to believe in God's love in general but it is very difficult to believe in God's love for me personally."[2] The love and acceptance of God is not hard to grasp from a global perspective. A young man once said to me, "Yes, I can believe that God loves and accepts all people, but I have a hard time believing that he accepts *me*." Why is this true for so many of us? Why do we find it easy to believe God accepts everyone else and hard to believe he accepts us? The answer is that we are filled with too much shame.

Ashamed in This Kingdom

From where does our shame come? As mentioned before, it comes from being a part of a fallen world. This is so crucial that I want to say it again. It is in the air we breathe. The kingdom of this world is diametrically opposed to the Kingdom of

God. The kingdom of this world values money, power, and sex appeal.

To live in the kingdom of this world is to be ashamed. We are valued and accepted only if we have money, hold positions of power, or are attractive and winsome. Therefore it is no surprise to see people chasing after wealth and status and beauty. Cosmetic surgery, hair weaves, diet pills, and liposuction are natural consequences of a world where external beauty counts for everything.

We feel shame if we do not have enough money. We feel unacceptable if we are too tall or too short, too fat or too thin. We feel shame if we work at a less-than-prestigious job or drive the wrong kind of car. We feel inferior if we do not have children, or if we have too many children. We feel unattractive if we do not have enough hair, or if we have too much hair. The reason we will always be ashamed in this kingdom is that there is always someone better, richer, more attractive, or smarter. No one can escape shame.

Responding to Shame

Many of us respond to this shame in three ways: puffing up, being good, or being bad. When I was in college I lived next door to a young man who had what his therapist called "a serious self-esteem problem." His recommended therapy was to listen to subliminal messages that told him over and over that he was good, attractive, valuable, smart, and important. While he slept, he listened to cassette tapes that showered him with praise. Unfortunately, it was a little like putting a band-aid on a deep flesh wound. It made him feel better about himself for a few moments, but not for long.

Another way to deal with shame is to be very good. We reason, "If I can be morally perfect, perhaps I can alleviate the shame." By being virtuous we just might convince ourselves we are acceptable. The problem is that when our acceptability is based on maintaining a flawless performance, we must struggle constantly and will inevitably fail.

The third way to deal with our sense of shame is to anesthetize it. We tire of constantly judging ourselves, monitoring our behavior, and manipulating every action, and our true self yearns to be free. In order to escape the pain we look to a pill or a bottle or a thrilling experience.

The anguish of shame cannot be escaped. We can be drenched with praise and applause and it still remains. We can be morally perfect, flawless in our actions, and it is still with us. We can take a pill and wait for the pain to subside, but it returns when the drug wears off. The agony cannot be escaped, but it can be healed.

The Truth About Who We Are

"Hey, fatty!" we would yell at one of the kids in my elementary class. We made fun of him, teased and taunted him about his size. He felt the pain of being the last one picked to play basketball. Mike will always remember being the only one in the class who didn't get any valentines—except for one from the teacher, who gave them to all of the class.

One day in junior high he sat behind me in gym class. Someone pushed him, and he fell on me. The kid who pushed him said Mike did it. With the whole class watching I was forced to either shrug it off or pick a fight. I chose the latter to retain my image as a tough guy. I said, "C'mon, man, let's fight." He said he didn't want to, but peer pressure forced him into a battle. He stood up and raised his fists like a boxer. With one punch I bloodied his nose. Just then the gym teacher came in. He saw us fighting and told us to go run a mile around the track.

But then he did something that changed me dramatically. He said with a smile, "I want you to run that mile holding each other's hands." The whole class roared in laughter. Embarrassed, Mike and I went out to the track and ran our mile. It was sometime on that cinder track that I remember looking at him, with his bloody nose and rotund body, and realizing that he was a person. We looked at each other and laughed. We actually became good friends. To this day I have never hit another person.

I no longer saw Mike as fat or stupid or ugly. I did not have to look past all of the externals, nor did I have to pretend he was valuable by focusing on his "good qualities." It was the truth about who he was, about who I was, that became real to me, jogging hand in hand with my bloody-nosed friend. It is the truth, and only the truth, that can set us free.

The Beast We Are

The old fairy tale about the beauty and the beast tells the story of how a beastly man hid behind a mask to prevent others from seeing his ugliness. When he was allowed to love and be loved he cautiously allowed the mask to be removed, only to find that he had become beautiful. If only life were more like fairy tales.

In reality you and I are a mess. Behind each of our masks is not a beautiful person. Behind the mask is a patchwork self that is more prone to lie than tell the truth, to take than give, to tear down than build up. When we look inside, really look, we may not like what we see.

Today, we live the lie that we are "pretty good" people who occasionally "make mistakes." The Christian doctrines of original sin and of human depravity have been replaced by a philosophy of original goodness and human potential. G. K. Chesterton noted, "Certain new theologians dispute original sin, which is the only part of Christian theology which can really be proved."[3]

We want to excuse our behavior and pretend that we are basically good and decent. I have noticed how shocked and horrified people are at their own sinfulness. In the midst of a confession I will often hear people say, "How could I have done such a thing?" Understanding our nature, "How could I not?" is the better question.

In his poem, "As the Ruin Falls," C. S. Lewis wrote, "I have never had a self-less thought since I was born."[4] Even at our best, Lewis believed, we are selfish. Our most noble acts, our highest virtues, are still tainted with self-interest.

The reason we have such trouble accepting ourselves as God accepts us is that we do not want to see ourselves as God sees us. God sees us as we truly are. He sees beneath the mask. In each of us he sees a scared person looking out for him- or herself, a person prone to making the wrong decision, a sinner capable of great sin.

When God looks at us he sees people who are both valuable and wicked. We are magnificent beings, so precious to God that he pursues us endlessly. We are also tainted by the Fall, influenced by the broken world in which we live, and susceptible to the lies of the enemy of our souls. There is something good in us, something God loves, but there is also something bad in us, something that only divine love can purge. We have enough depravity in us that we will never be able to save ourselves.

Obsessed by Our Own Insignificance

In his play *The Cocktail Party,* T. S. Eliot gets beneath the surface of our misguided attempts to find self-acceptance. One of the characters, Edward, is a boorish, alcoholic adulterer who has finally found his pain unbearable. He meets a stranger at a cocktail party, a man he does not know, and for some reason begins sharing his feelings of inadequacy. He tells the man that he is afraid, afraid that deep down he is "ridiculous."

"It will do you no harm to find yourself ridiculous," the stranger tells him. "Resign yourself to be the fool you are. That's the best advice I can give you." Edward later finds out that the stranger at the party is actually a psychiatrist. Hoping to get at the problem of his own insecurity, he visits him at his office.

"I am obsessed by the thought of my own insignificance," he tells the psychiatrist.

"Precisely," the doctor replies. "And I could make you feel important, and you would imagine it a marvelous cure; and you would go on, doing such amount of mischief as lay within your power—until you came to grief. Half of the harm that is done in this world is due to the people who want to feel important . . . because *they are absorbed in the endless struggle to think well of themselves.*"[5]

We want so badly to think well of ourselves, not knowing that the answer to our struggle is to let go of the need to feel important. Eliot is right when he notes that it is an endless struggle, endless because we will never be able to think well of ourselves. Why? God never intended us to. Like running on a treadmill, we expend a great deal of energy and actually go nowhere.

As long as we continue to try to think well of ourselves we will have to distort reality. We will have to believe a lie. We will have to create a facade, participate in a charade, and avoid looking closely at our true selves. We will wear ourselves out trying to convince ourselves that we are something that we are not.

Real Humility

The truth of the matter is that I am a bundle of paradoxes. If I watch myself closely in brutal honesty, I see that I am capable of lying, cheating, stealing, fantasizing, using others, and hating people who have more than I. And all that before noon. I am no stranger to pride, envy, anger, laziness, greed, and lust.

I am also capable of doing good to people, making a selfless sacrifice for another, and having the good sense to keep quiet about it. I am capable of telling the truth, of behaving in a moral way, and of standing up for the cause of justice. I have had moments of real humility, peace, joy, and love.

St. Francis of Assisi, it is said, considered himself the worst of all sinners, even though he was renowned for his moral life and works of charity. When asked how he could say this of himself when it was obvious there were more immoral persons than he, St. Francis replied, "If God had blessed them with such great mercy as he has blessed me, they would acknowledge God's gifts much more than I do and serve him better than I do, and if my God would abandon me I would commit more misdeeds than any other man."[6]

His words sound foreign to modern ears. We would rather declare St. Francis a neurotic than admit that maybe, just maybe, he might be right. Perhaps the solution to our problem of shame is not to try to think better of ourselves or to think worse of ourselves. Perhaps the answer is to think rightly about ourselves.

Becoming a Realist

Jesus told a story about a religious man and a man whom society deemed a sinner simply by his occupation as a tax collector, who both went up to the temple to pray (see Luke 18:9–14). The religious man prayed a prayer of thanksgiving to God that he was such a pious person. The other man stood off in the distance, afraid to get near God's holy temple. He fell to his knees and prayed, "God be merciful to me, a sinner." Jesus says that one of the two men went home in favor with God. Which one? The one who was honest. The one who cried out in need.

Evelyn Underhill, commenting on this passage, notes,

> The publican's desperate sense of need and imperfection made instant contact with the source of all perfection. . . . He had got the thing in proportion. We need not suppose he was a specially wicked man; but he knew he was an imperfect, dependent, needy man, without any claims or any rights. *He was a realist.* That opened a channel, and started a communion, between the rich God and the poor soul.[7]

In order for us to begin the process of self-acceptance we will have to acknowledge our true selves. We do not need to beat ourselves up, or call ourselves names, or excessively confess our sinfulness. All we have to do is be realistic.

We are imperfect. We are highly dependent. We have no claims and no rights. We are sinners. And that is a good thing, considering the fact that Jesus said, "I have come to call not the righteous but sinners" (Matt. 9:13). Pretending that we are righteous simply keeps God at bay and delays our healing.

St. Paul knew who he was, and therefore he relied all the more on God's grace. He even went so far as to say that he would *boast* of his weaknesses (2 Cor. 12:5–10). The truth that we must accept if we are to be healed is the truth that we are weak and broken and imperfect, for that is who we are.

The inability to be weak before God is the nemesis of the spiritual life. Paul would often boast, but not of his own abilities, his wisdom, or his accomplishments. He proudly proclaimed all that God had done and was doing in him. Paul was proud, not of himself but of God. The more he realized his weakness, the less he relied on his own effort, thus allowing God to become more and more powerful in his life. God's love and acceptance rested on him, a man who did not deserve it. Consequently, he made his life a gift back to God.

Liberation Through Truth

The gospel is good news to the broken and contrite, to the sick who are in need of a physician. We lack community in many churches precisely because we have been ashamed to admit that we are sick. Admitting the truth of who we really are is the first step to building real community.

Dietrich Bonhoeffer, Lutheran pastor and theologian of our century, put it well:

> It is the grace of the gospel which is so hard for the pious to understand, that it confronts us with the truth and says: You are a sinner, a great and desperate sinner; now come, as the sinner that you are, to God who loves you. He wants you as you are; He does not want anything from you, a sacrifice, a work; He wants you alone. 'My son, give me thine heart' (Prov. 23:26). God has come to you to save the sinner. Be glad! This message is liberation through truth. . . . You do not have to go on lying to yourself and your brothers, as if you were without sin; you can dare to be a sinner.[8]

Now we can stop lying to ourselves. We are saved from our own self-deception the moment we say with the tax collector, "God be merciful to me, *a sinner*" (Luke 18:13). We no longer need to apply cosmetics to make ourselves more acceptable to God. We have been accepted by God, and therefore, we can accept ourselves.

Self-Improvement Versus Self-Surrender

The path of our healing is not one of self-improvement, but rather, of self-surrender.[9] Trying to improve our existing selves is precisely our problem. When we cease from the battle of trying to think well of ourselves and turn to God in complete nakedness, we will find nothing but acceptance.

We may fear that God will draw away from us if we are honest, but in fact the opposite movement occurs. God is able to draw near to us the moment we surrender our need to control how he feels about us through our behavior. "Here I am, God. You know I am broken and wayward and foolish." These words dismantle our pride and allow God to penetrate our hearts.

All that really matters is being sincere about who we are. This is liberating in that we can now concentrate on the relationship that God has established with us through Christ. We can take our eyes off of ourselves and our vain notions of perfection and simply accept our failures and faults, not excusing them but seeing them as a part of who we are. We can then walk with Christ. We can take our eyes off of the carefully laid plans of holiness we have conceived; our focus now is on the present God who has drawn near to us in our honesty, our poverty, and our need.

God Is Greater Than Our Hearts

God has chosen to accept what we deem unacceptable. The parts of us that cause us shame do not shame God. Here is the Good News: even if we feel condemned by our own hearts, God is greater than our hearts. The apostle John wrote:

> And by this we will know that we are from the truth and will reassure our hearts before him *whenever our hearts condemn us;* for *God is greater than our hearts,* and he knows everything. Beloved, if our hearts do not condemn us, we have boldness before God (1 John 3:19–21).

We may feel deep shame, and we may condemn ourselves unmercifully, but God does not. And if God does not condemn us, then who are we to condemn ourselves? Are we greater than God? Is our insight greater than God's?

God's acceptance should lead us to self-acceptance. Grace heals our shame not by trying to find something good and lovely within us that is worth loving but by looking at us as we are, the good and the bad, the lovely and the unlovely, and simply accepting us. God accepts us with the promise that we will never be unacceptable to him. Now it is ours to do the same for ourselves.

Removing the Fear

God heals us by removing the core of our shame: the fear of rejection. When we are honest with God, when our souls have been laid bare, and we experience his acceptance, the fear of abandonment subsides. God did not leave us. Now it is ours to extend that acceptance to ourselves, to take ownership of ourselves.

The sign that we are being healed of our shame comes the moment we are able to say, "I am imperfect, I am broken, and I am weak. But God accepts me, and therefore *I* can accept myself. He did not turn away when I showed him my scars and warts, but he reached down and kissed them. I am who I am before God."

Our need to appear good will subside, and we will finally be able "to move freely in the mystery of who we really are."[10] God has made me a human being. That was his design. For too long I thought God made a mistake in this regard. I used to think God would prefer me to be more like a robot, faultless and perfect in every move. My humanity was something I tried to escape. I used to pray that God would take it away: "Lord, to err is human—help me be something other than human." But my humanity does not appear to bother God. By growing in his grace I have learned to embrace it, to give thanks for it. It is who I am.

It took me a long time to grasp the truth of what the Spanish composer Pablo Casals once said, "The main thing in life is not to be afraid to be human."[11] God's acceptance has enabled me to enjoy my humanity. I am free from the bondage of taking myself so seriously. As Chesterton once noted, "Angels can fly because they take themselves lightly."[12] Embracing my humanity is enabling me to fly.

We Are What We Are

In the wisdom of Popeye, I can boldly proclaim, "I am what I am." This is true no matter what I or other people say. If someone praises me, I am what I am. If someone criticizes me, I am what I am. No amount of praise or blame can make me other than what I am.

What really matters is what God says about us. What would it matter if a thousand people bowed before us and praised our name if God condemned us? What would it matter if ten thousand people reviled and cursed us if God accepted and loved us? We have already been accepted by the one whose acceptance is all that really matters.

God's acceptance of me as I am allows me to accept myself as I am. In fact, not to accept myself would be to deny God's word, to reject God's voice, the voice that tells me I am his "Beloved."[13] We are able to accept ourselves only on

God's terms. His acceptance of us is not based on any qualities we possess. Trying to build a proper self-image on those grounds would surely collapse. But his acceptance is a promise, and therefore it is received through an act of faith.

Perhaps *trust* is the better word. Just as a child trusts in his or her parents' acceptance, not based on performance but on the basis of being a child, so too we are being called to become children again. We are learning to trust. We are urged to make peace with our flawed existence and, even more, to risk that the mystery of our being is trustworthy.

May we have the courage not to run when the voice of our condemning heart would tear us from the place where we can hear the voice of God saying to us, "You are my beloved child, in whom I am well pleased." Even if our hearts condemn us, God is greater than our hearts.

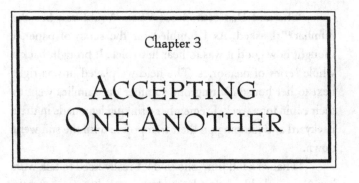

Chapter 3

ACCEPTING ONE ANOTHER

Beloved, since God loved us so much,
we also ought to love one another.

1 JOHN 4:11

When my wife handed me the phone I asked her, "Who is it?"

"I don't know. I don't recognize the voice," she said.

"Hello, this is Jim," I said. And then a voice I knew but had not heard for years began to speak.

"This is Marge, remember me? Of course you do. You grew up with my boys. We still live in the same house, behind the one you grew up in. Say, I was trying to reach your mother. Where is she living now?"

"She and Dad retired out West. Would you like the number?" I asked. As I fumbled for the scrap of paper, I thought how good it was to hear her voice. It brought back a whole series of memories. The field we played in was right next to her house. During one summer our families went to their cabin for a week. I remember drinking lemonade in their backyard and jumping on their trampoline until the sun went down.

"Thanks a lot, Jim," she said. "I really need to talk with her. You probably didn't know, but our oldest son recently died."

"Oh, no Marge, I didn't hear. I am sorry to hear that," I said in shock.

"He died of complications with the AIDS virus. I just needed to talk to your mom. She was always so accepting. No matter what happens I know I can always call her and she will stand by me. I love your mom so much."

We spoke for a few minutes longer and then I hung up, wondering why, after ten years, this woman would try to reach my mother. Then it hit me. "No matter what happens," her voice echoed inside of me, "I know I can always call her and she will stand by me." Suddenly I understood. She knew that she could be honest with my mother and find on the other end of the line a person who would accept her and comfort her.

In a time of great anguish we look for a person who will welcome us, who will not be shocked or bothered by our struggles and failures, who will listen to us and receive all that we have in our hearts. When we find such a person we cling to them and give thanks for them. They are all too rare.

Acceptance Is Contagious

People who demonstrate pure acceptance say with their eyes, as well as their voice, that we are free to be who we are. There is no need to pretend around these people, no need to put on airs. They communicate nonverbally: "It's okay. I like you. You do not have to impress me."

I will hear people say of a certain person, "I can really be myself around her," or, "I find myself opening up to him." We feel accepted with these kinds of people, and the pressure to be something other than what we are is gone.

They are treating others the way God treats all of us. They receive God's love, appropriate and accept it for themselves, and naturally extend it to other people. They are conduits of God's love. They are carrying the virus of acceptance, and everyone they meet seems to catch it.

My mother is not a psychologist or a professional counselor; she simply radiates real and genuine acceptance. Because of this people flock to her. Marge, in her time of suffering, needed to feel accepted by someone she could trust, and she was willing to search the country to find that person. We all desire acceptance, to feel the love of God flowing out of a person; it is the silent yearning of our hearts.

Why Is It Hard to Love?

The amazing thing about acceptance is that it isn't something *we* do. It is something that is done to us, and if we let it run its natural course, it will spread in ever-widening circles.

Unconditional acceptance cannot be forced. People sense in a minute when acceptance is contrived.

Not all of us are capable of extending this kind of acceptance to others. Usually this is because there is too much pain in our lives. A psychiatrist was once asked how a person learns to love. He responded by saying that people who are in pain tend to focus on their own problems. When we have a toothache it is hard to think of anything else except the pain. The psychiatrist noted, "Most human beings are so turned in by their own pains that they cannot get enough out of themselves to love to any great extent."[1]

This is why it is so crucial that we understand and accept God's acceptance of us. Only then will we be able to "get enough out of" ourselves. We may still have pain, but once we have found rest in our own acceptance—as we are, not as we should be—we will begin to see others in the same light.

As We Love Ourselves

The way I love others is a direct reflection of how I love myself. If I am ruthless with myself, exact with my judgment, and prone to condemn myself, I will be the same toward others. When Jesus said we are to love our neighbors as ourselves he was not so much stating a proposition as a fact. We *do* love our neighbors as ourselves.

When God graciously revealed himself to me as a God of acceptance, it took me several years to begin to internalize and appropriate it. I still have moments of doubt. But once I began to trust in God's acceptance of me I noticed that it immediately influenced the way I dealt with others. As I began to feel loved, I began reaching out to others in love; as I learned to believe that I was chosen, I found myself wanting to tell everyone that they, too, were chosen.

I began to see ministry as a matter of reconciliation. I believe this was how Paul viewed ministry: "All this is from God, who reconciled us to himself through Christ, and has given us *the ministry of reconciliation*" (2 Cor. 5:18). Everywhere I go I meet people who feel alienated from God, and it is a special privilege to tell them about God's acceptance. Ministry became easier when I realized that *I* do not have a ministry, but rather, I am simply an extension of Christ's ministry to the world.

We Love as We Are Loved

The fact that God is loving toward us leads us to be loving toward one another. That is the foundation of all genuine love. God is a loving God, and those who would live in him will by necessity become loving people.

One day chatting over coffee a friend asked me, "Jim, how do you know that you are a Christian?"

"Well, I guess I would have to say that I know it deep down inside. I don't really have any way to prove it. It is just something I know, and I know that I know," I answered, somewhat confused.

"It seems to me," he said, "that the only real proof that we have, the only evidence there is of Christ's presence in us, is the *compassion* we show to other people."

I knew that he was right. Real, genuine tenderness toward other people is the only indication we have that Christ lives in us. Jesus said, "By this everyone will know that you are my disciples, if you have love for one another" (John 13:35).

We are able to love because God first loved us (1 John 4:19). We are simply channels of his acceptance. Our love for one another is a continuation of God's love for us. If we find ourselves unable to demonstrate love and acceptance, it may be that we do not feel loved and accepted ourselves. We have not yet accepted God's acceptance and love for us.

What God's Love Is Like

God is love, we read in the Bible. But what does that mean? What is God's love like? In 1 Corinthians 13:4–8 we have one of the most beautiful descriptions of what love is: it is patient and kind, it is not boastful or rude, keeps no record of wrongs, hopes all things, believes all things, and never ends.

This is what God's love toward us is like. God is patient—he puts up with our faults and failures without grumbling. God is kind—he does not seek to coerce or control us. God is not boastful—he does not need to impress us. God is not rude—he never needs to offend or manipulate us. God keeps no record of wrongs—he does not keep an account of our mistakes so that he may one day judge us. God hopes and believes—he sees our potential even when we doubt and despair of ourselves.

If God is this way with us, then as extensions of his life in us, we, too, can offer this kind of love to those around us. God has put up with my stupidity and lack of faith, and continued to reach out to me, and this enables me to do the same with my brothers and sisters. God has chosen not to condemn me, to force his will upon me, or to give up on me, even when I have given up on myself. Now I can do the same for someone else. When we offer this kind of love to those around us we enable them to become something beautiful.

No Strain in Love

We should not have to strain and struggle to reach out to one another with this kind of acceptance. When we look at a branch bearing fruit we would never say, "Wow, look at the effort of that branch! It must be working hard to produce that fruit." The branch is able to bear the fruit because it is attached to the vine, not because of its effort.

In the same way, loving others is not a matter of will-power but of Christ's life and power flowing through us. Peter van Breeman writes, "Christian love is God himself or, in other words, sharing in that love which is God himself. We have only to open wide our hearts and love will flow in and through us to others. We are simply channels for his love. There is no strain in love."[2]

Christian love is Christ's love forcing its way out of our hearts and into our hands and feet and thoughts and words. When we discover that God has accepted us we will eventually come to see that God has accepted all people in the same manner. When we come to see our neighbors with full acceptance we will suddenly realize that we are seeing them with Christ's eyes.

This is the work of the Holy Spirit within us. The chief function of the Holy Spirit, writes spiritual leader Thomas Merton, is to "draw us into the mystery of the incarnation and of our redemption by the Word made flesh. He not only makes us understand something of God's love as it is manifested to us in Christ, but He also makes us live by that love and experience it in our hearts."[3]

So, it is by the work of the Holy Spirit in us that we are able to love and accept one another on the terms that we have been loved and accepted. Therefore, we can say that it is not we who love, but *it is God who loves them in us*. Jesus is the vine, and we are merely the branches (John 15:5). Apart from him we cannot love.

Who Do You Love?

Early in his ministry, Jesus confronted the question, "Who am I obligated to love?" The common belief among many of the Jewish teachers was that one was required only to love one's neighbors, which meant only fellow Jews. Jesus was asked by a man, "Who is my neighbor?" He answered this question by telling a story about a man who had been robbed and beaten and was helped only by a Samaritan (Luke 10:30–37). Jesus shocked his hearers by making a Samaritan—a race of people hated by most Jews in that day—the hero of the story. In so doing he erased the lines of exclusion his hearers had drawn when deciding who, and who not, to love.

Jesus does the same for us today. We draw lines of exclusion based on race, status, religion, and gender, and Jesus erases them. When we find that we have been accepted regardless of our color or creed, we are moved to do the same with others. If we have been comprehensively accepted, then we must accept others comprehensively. No one is unacceptable in God's eyes. We are called to have the same vision.

God loves the least of the brethren (Matt. 25) and so can we. God loves those we foolishly call our enemies, and so can we. The real litmus test of our willingness to accept others comes when we ask, "Do I draw lines of inclusion and exclusion, or does my love and acceptance include all people—the greatest and the least?"

How Do We Love?

How do I show this kind of acceptance to my neighbor? The better question is, How has Jesus shown acceptance to me? The way he loves us is a reflection of how we are to love others, for he said, "Just *as I have loved you,* you also should love one another" (John 13:34).

A large part of acceptance is letting people be who they are, with all of their uniqueness, all of their beauty, all of their flaws. I find this easier to say than to do. I have a terrible habit of looking at a person as someone I can help, rather than as someone I can accept and love. "I wonder what he struggles with," I will say to myself. Then I reason about how I can fix him. I have learned that I can do more for others by trying *not* to fix them and by accepting them wholesale.

It is no crime to want the best for people. My problem comes when I create an agenda or carve out an ideal that I want someone to live up to. I am not accepting when I do this, and often I am wrong about what the person should be or what the person should do with his or her own life. My first and primary objective must be to accept people as they are.

If I wait for others to be what I want them to be, I will never accept them. By looking at what my brother is *not,* instead of at what he *is,* I will never be able to sympathize with him, struggle with him, hurt with him, or rejoice with him.

What I can do is enter into the mystery of who that person is. St. Paul once wrote, "we regard no one from a human standpoint" (2 Cor. 5:16). The world we live in judges people from a "human standpoint," putting them in classes and castes, revering the rich and despising the poor. Paul and his fellow Christians did not look at people as rich or poor, beautiful or ugly, strong or weak, young or old; they regarded all people as valuable. Why? There is not a living soul for whom Jesus did not die.

We sometimes fear that certain people are too highly regarded; too much respect is given to celebrities and athletes and political figures. I think the real problem is not that we revere some people too much, it is that *we revere each other too little.* Every person we will meet today is a walking miracle, if only we have the eyes of faith to see it.

Loving the Weakness

I tend to look at another person and ask myself, "What is the good I can find in him, so that I can accept him?" or, "What wonderful qualities does she possess that I can discover, so that I can value her?" I am learning to take the opposite route, starting instead with what is unacceptable in the eyes of the world. I am striving to look at others and ask, "I wonder if there is some pain, some weakness, some struggle, that I can discover and identify with, so that I can accept this person."

It sounds preposterous, and yet this is exactly how God reaches out to us. God looks not to our strengths but to our weaknesses as a means of inserting his love into our hearts. If we are to accept one another, it will begin not with our gifts and strengths but with our faults and our weaknesses.

I am learning not to discount people because of their weaknesses nor to regard them for their strengths. The proper response to anyone we meet is both skepticism and awe. By accepting the negative aspects, the dark sides, of one another, we accept one another as God accepts us. Real, genuine acceptance begins at the point of weakness.

In so doing we draw out the goodness that is in other people. There is no fear, no danger of rejection, no possibility of being cast aside. The negative has already been dealt with. Now there is an opportunity for the hidden wonder of each person to emerge. As Frederick Buechner notes, "It is not until we love a person in all his ugliness that we can make him beautiful, or ourselves either."[4]

The Rescuing Spirit of Love

Once we have been drenched in God's complete acceptance of who we are and have taken ownership of ourselves in light of our dark side, I believe we become more useful to God. God has used certain people who possess this kind of acceptance to change the course of history.

Evelyn Underhill mentions a few: "Think of St. Francis with his special selfless love for lepers, or St. Catherine of Sienna saying, 'I will take your sins upon me'; or Father

Wainright, of whom it is said, 'You must be either a drunkard or a criminal to know him well.' What were their lives but this—channels for the rescuing Spirit of Love?"[5]

God invests his love in us so that we might become for others, as Thomas Merton put it, "a *sacrament* of the mysterious and infinitely selfless love God has for them."[6] To be sure, it is a divine gift to be able to accept one another as God accepts us. Merton's use of the word "sacrament" is fitting in that we become an outward and visible sign of an inward and spiritual grace.

A Medal of Honor

One summer I worked as a chaplain in a retirement home. I found out quickly that one man, Earl, would monopolize at least one hour each day. He would invite me to his room for coffee, and then proceed to weep for the next hour or so about the loss of his wife. She wasn't dead, but she had a severe case of Alzheimer's disease and did not even recognize him.

He would hold my hand, squeezing it harder and harder as he sobbed about his dear Lilah, who lived in the building next door but was thousands of miles away. Each day I dreaded visiting Earl. His room smelled awful. Earl smelled awful, too. I knew that I was just a warm body filling his recliner; anyone who would listen would do. Like a mannequin I sat motionless and silent, holding his hand, for one hour each day.

He did not want my advice. I could not solve his problems anyway. There was no solution, there was only the suffering, the waiting, and the despairing.

"I am sick of visiting Earl," I said to my supervisor.

"He needs you, Jim. Don't you know that?" she said.

"He needs anyone who will listen. It just happens to be my job to do that. He doesn't really need *me*," I protested.

"Yes, he does. It's just that you can't see it. He loves you because you are there. You don't have the answers, Jim, but you have your presence to give him and that is all he needs. Your presence is Jesus' presence to him," she concluded emphatically.

When the summer ended I made my last visit to Earl's room. I was so glad to have ended my tour of duty. He let me in and gave me one last cup of coffee. Then he went into his room. When he came out he was holding a box containing a medal he had won in the war. I remembered him talking about it many times. It was the symbol of his life's achievement and the thing of which he was most proud.

"I want you to have this," he said.

"Oh, no, Earl," I said with a note of shock. "I could never take this. But thank you for offering it to me."

"You will never know how much it meant to me to have you visit each day. It was all I had to hang on to. You never judged me, and you listened to me go on and on—you even let me blubber like a baby. I can never repay you. Please, take this . . . for me," he said.

I never let him give me his medal. He was the one who earned a medal of valor; I had only earned a badge of self-centeredness. He was the one who endured the real battle, the battle of loneliness and fear and grief. I went home each evening to my family and friends, to laughter and hope. Earl went to bed with his tears.

My job that summer was to minister to Earl, but in the end it was he who ministered to me. Jesus said when we visit the sick, the imprisoned, and the lonely (Earl was all three), we are really visiting him (see Matt. 25). Years later as I recall that summer chaplaincy I cannot remember anything other than Earl.

Acceptance Does Not Overlook Faults

To offer a person complete and utter acceptance does not mean that we are to overlook that person's faults, to excuse bad behavior, or to deny that person's defects. In order to offer genuine acceptance we must know about the dark side, but knowing does not mean condoning.

I do not want my brothers and sisters to excuse my sin. If they chose to overlook my faults or rationalize my short-comings, they would not be loving me. I need people who will hope for me always, expect much from me, and yearn for me to be as whole and complete as I can be. To accept me as I am and then leave me as I am is not love, but apathy.

"My true brothers," wrote St. Augustine, "are those who rejoice for me in their hearts when they find good in me, and grieve for me when they find sin. They are my true brothers, because whether they see good in me or evil, they love me still. To such as these I shall reveal what I am."[7]

The Economy of Love

Being able to accept one another is a divine gift. It begins with God's reaching out to us and accepting us unconditionally. Divine acceptance will then fill our hearts until we can take possession of this acceptance for ourselves. Finally, this acceptance will move out from our hearts and into our lives, spilling over on everyone we meet.

God's love for us is without limit. In the economy of divine love we will discover that the more we give, the more we have to give. I have noticed that no matter how much I try, I cannot exhaust God's love. I have never seen it run out. But I can only give as much as I have received, and the measure of love I receive is in direct proportion to how much I desire to know it, feel it, and give it away.

Paul used the metaphor of a jar made of clay that has been filled with an enormous treasure to describe the Christian life: "We have this treasure in clay jars, so that it may be made clear that this extraordinary power belongs to God and does not come from us" (2 Cor. 4:7). You and I are simply jars. The jar itself is not what really matters. What is important is the treasure inside.

We may not feel like we have the capacity to accept one another unconditionally. We are right. We do not have the ability to love as God loves. But thank God we do not have to conjure up this kind of acceptance. All we have to do is carry God's acceptance to the people around us. "Look at this treasure, this wealth, that is for you," we say to one another. In giving it away we will find that, far from diminishing the treasure within us, it has increased.

PART TWO

RECEIVING
GOD'S
FORGIVENESS

Chapter 4

GOD'S FORGIVENESS

*Divine forgiveness makes a heroic demand upon
our courage. For that forgiveness is not the easy passing
of a sponge over a slate. It is a stern and painful process:
it means the re-ordering of the soul's disordered love,
setting right what is wrong, washing it from
wickedness and cleansing it from sin.*

EVELYN UNDERHILL

My friend, Rich Mullins, was once hiking the Appalachian trail when he happened upon a young man who offered him a ride to the next camp. After a long ride and an even longer talk the man said to Rich, "Well, I should probably tell you that I am gay."

"Oh, well, I should probably tell you that I am a Christian," Rich replied.

"Do you want to get out of the car now that you know this about me?" the young man asked.

"No. If I enjoyed your company before I knew that, why should it change now."

"Well, I just thought that Christians hated gays."

"I thought Christians loved everyone," Rich responded.

"Well, I thought God hated gays."

"And I thought God is love. I am not aware of any parameters on that," Rich said. A few moments of silence passed between them as they drove ahead into the darkness. With a serious and somber voice the young man asked, "Do you think that I will go to hell for being gay?"

Rich started to say yes. Everything in him wanted to say, "Yes. Of course you'll go to hell for being gay." But something incredible happened. Even Rich was shocked and surprised at the words that rolled off his tongue:

"No, you won't go to hell for being gay," Rich heard his voice say. Stunned at what had just come out of his own mouth—despite what his mind had informed his mouth to speak—he wondered from where such an answer came.

Rich worried that he might have given the young man permission to do something that God had not give him permission to do. But at the same moment a realization came over him. His mind was awakened to a statement so real and so true that it echoed throughout his heart as he spoke: "You won't go to hell for being gay anymore than someone else would go to hell for being a liar, or a thief, or a racist. The reason a person goes to hell," Rich went on, "is because that person rejects the grace and the forgiveness that God longs to give every one of us."

The young man began weeping. "I have never heard anything like that before in my life," he said. The two parted as friends.

When Rich told me the story I thought about how the message of the gospel is not real until it intersects with our lives. Most people only *think* they have heard the gospel, when in fact they have never really heard it at all. We often think we have heard the Good News of God's complete acceptance and forgiveness and care, and yet, until that is tested in the grit and reality of human existence, it remains a pious platitude.

Acceptance and Forgiveness

That young man needed to hear that he was accepted by God before he could begin to grasp his forgiveness. I believe we must know that we are unconditionally loved and accepted by God before we can deal with the issue of our sins. Peter van Breeman notes, "When we really accept God's acceptance and believe that it is without limits, then we can express our guilt."[1]

The young man felt accepted enough after their long drive to share his painful secret of being gay. When Rich did not reject him, it allowed the young man to probe deeper into the issue that was troubling him. Knowing that we are accepted enables us to bring our painful failures to the surface where God can begin to heal them.

When I began to believe, really believe, that I was accepted by God *as I am,* I suddenly felt the freedom to explore my dark side in a way I had not known. Before I began to understand that God loved and accepted all of me I was unable to allow God to enter into my struggle. Paralyzed by my fear of rejection, I kept my sins hidden and in the dark. As long as evil remains in the dark it holds a power over us. If, by God's grace, we are able to bring our sins to the light, we see that they lose their power.

We All Struggle

This is why the enemy of our souls strives to keep us from confessing and sharing our struggle, with God or with one another. There are misconceptions—subtle lies—that when believed will keep us from sharing who we are. The first one is this: "I am the only one who struggles." We are foolish if we believe that we are the only person who has ever battled this or that vice.

I remember being in a discipleship group with several young men. For several weeks we shared only the acceptable offenses: getting a little angry, feeling discouraged, telling a white lie. But then one of the members took a risk and shared a real and ongoing struggle with sin. No one judged him, and in fact, each one of us made him feel accepted and thanked him for sharing. Then, one by one, each of us opened up and confessed our own struggles.

A second misconception sounds something like this: "After you become a Christian you should never fall to temptation because Jesus has saved you from sin." Brennan Manning tells people in his testimony that he became an alcoholic *after* he became a priest. Brennan notes that many people are surprised by this, wondering how it is possible that a person could get caught up in a sin or an addiction *after* that person has been "saved." Brennan writes,

It is possible because I got battered and bruised by lone-liness and failure, because I got discouraged, uncertain, guilt-ridden, and took my eyes off of Jesus. Because the Christ encounter did not transfigure me into an angel. Because justification by grace through faith means I have been set in right relationship with God, not made the equivalent of a patient etherized on a table.[2]

When we respond to God's grace and move into his glorious acceptance, we will still fail. Knowing and loving Jesus does not make us immune from vice.

We all struggle. Every person I know wrestles with the conflict between the Spirit and the flesh, as Paul described it (Rom. 8:4–13). It does not end when we believe in Jesus, and in fact, it could be said that the war only begins after we come to the faith. No one is exempt from this internal war.

Our Faces May Not Betray Us

I once was on a retreat with a group of pastors and church leaders. We met for two days of teaching and lively discussion. We chatted over coffee and took walks together, learning a lit-tle bit about who we were. On the final evening we decided to have a communion service. One of the leaders suggested we offer an opportunity for people to come for a private prayer of anointing, to let them share any hurts or confess any sins. I said, "Do you think anyone will come? I mean, these are all church leaders. I can't imagine they would want to do this."

That evening nearly everyone at the retreat came for a time of private confession. I had no idea they were struggling, as I am sure they had no idea I was fighting and losing internal battles as well. Our faces never betrayed us. They shared their shortcomings and faults, their past mistakes and present demons, sometimes in detail, and I simply listened. Then I anointed their foreheads with oil in the sign of the cross and announced their forgiveness. One of them offered the same opportunity for me, and I was able to bring some things to the light with which I had been struggling.

Our faces looked different after that time. They shined. Later that night I thought of how all of us—literally all of us—struggle with sin. One thing was strange: even though I could remember their faces, I could not remember their sins. I suppose God couldn't either.

Why We Hide

When we feel alone in our struggle, we will find ourselves hiding not only from one another but also from God. Yet we will also be reluctant to turn to God after we commit a shameful act if we fear that we will be scolded and punished. It is better to avoid God, we reason, than to face his fury. This, too, is a misconception that prevents us from walking in freedom and enjoying our life with God. We end up hiding from the one who longs to heal us and, in fact, is the only one who *can* heal us.

Adam and Eve hid from God after they did what they knew they were not supposed to do. God knew where they were, but went looking for them anyway, calling out, "Adam, where are you?" God was so tender and gracious toward them that he even bent down and made them clothes to cover their newly discovered nakedness (see Gen. 3:8).

We hide when we feel threatened or uncertain as to how we will be treated. One icy morning when I was in high school, I lost control of the car and brushed past a tree, leaving a mark on the bumper. I was afraid to tell my dad because I thought sure he would lecture me about being careful behind the wheel or, worse, that he would ground me. When I finally did tell him he was not upset about the car but was worried about my well-being. More important, he was hurt that I did not feel that I could tell him. "Never be afraid to come to me, Jim. I love you no matter what you do."

A Forgiving God

This is how God feels when we are afraid to go to him with any and all things we have done. If we assume he is going to punish us, we do not know God. God cares more about us than about what we have done. Too many of us have lived with the misconception that God would rather condemn than forgive, and as a result we have lost the joy of living honestly and freely before a loving heavenly Father.

God is a forgiving God. In fact, God *loves* to forgive. Whenever we—in our freedom—assert our independence and run from God, God—in his compassion—finds a way to bring us home. "At the heart of God is the desire to give and forgive," writes Richard Foster.[3]

God is more eager to forgive us than we are to be forgiven. I think of how many times I have pulled away from a relationship with God, sulking after committing some sin, afraid to come home. Each and every time I did come home God was already there, welcoming me, forgiving, desiring nothing other than my presence.

Jesus gave us a beautiful description of God's desire to forgive in the parable of the prodigal son (Luke 15:11–32). When the wayward son finally comes to his senses and decides to return home to the father he has rejected, he expects judgment but receives mercy instead:

> I will get up and go to my father, and I will say to him, "Father, I have sinned against heaven and before you; I am no longer worthy to be called your son; treat me like one of your hired hands." So he set off and went to his father. But while he was still far off, his father saw him and was filled with compassion; he ran and put his arms around him and kissed him (Luke 15:18–20).

We often fear, like the son, that to return to God will mean certain punishment. But God, who is like this father, is "filled with compassion" when he sees us return, and he runs to meet us, to embrace us and kiss us.

The Forgiveness Established by God

God loves us so much that he forgives us even before we ask for forgiveness. That is what I see when I look at the cross. Even before we were born God was reconciling himself to us through the sacrifice of his Son. Why did God do this? Why did God have to die? In order to understand the forgiveness established by God we must turn to the Bible.

When God gathered the people of Israel out of the dust of the desert he established a covenant with them, an agree-

nation for those who are in Christ Jesus" (Rom. 8:1). God came down to us and made peace, wiping away our guilt and removing any and all condemnation.

There is no need for more sacrifices, no need for more blood to be shed. Jesus' single death on the cross was sufficient for all time. This frees us from having to establish our own forgiveness, from having to worry from day to day about our status before God. In Christ we do not do anything to receive forgiveness; it is a gift God gives to any and all who accept it.

Receiving God's Forgiveness

There is nothing that we have done or can do to earn this forgiveness, and this is precisely what causes many of us to reject it. We often prefer to be in control, to show that we are worthy, and to prove that we deserve to be forgiven. God's forgiveness cannot be earned, no matter how hard we try, but there is still something in us that wants to try.

Coming to believe in God's complete and final forgiveness was not an easy process for me. At first I thought it was too good to be true. I could not understand how someone could offer forgiveness without some act of contrition or promise of restitution. The major obstacle to receiving God's forgiveness is our unwillingness to accept God's offer *as it is*. We like to add to it, modify and adjust it, to make it more realistic.

After all, who would forgive us once and for all? Who would forgive us even before we sinned against them? Who would forgive us even before we asked for forgiveness? Only

God is able to do that. I had to come to the point where I needed to let go of my own standards and simply accept God's gracious invitation.

I think it was my pride that hurt the most. As long as I had my own method for getting forgiven, *I* was in control. Accepting God's offer of forgiveness humbled me because I could do nothing to earn it. All I could do was stand in awe, which, incidentally, is a good place to stand.

The Promise and the Path

If a person asks me, "Jim, how do you know you are forgiven?" I can only point to the cross. I cannot rely on my own feelings, nor can I explain it logically: "For the message about the cross is foolishness to those who are perishing, but to us who are being saved it is the power of God" (1 Cor. 1:18). God's forgiveness is a *promise* made to us, but it takes time for us to let it sink in.

Receiving God's offer of forgiveness does not happen overnight. We need to spend time soaking ourselves in it, letting it seep from our minds into our hearts. The Christian life is like a *path* in that we are on a journey of discovery. Along the way we catch glimpses of the promises and begin to appropriate them. God's forgiveness is a solid fact on which we can rely, but it must be realized in the fiction of our everyday lives.

John Wesley, the eighteenth-century theologian who founded Methodism, lived as a Christian for thirty-five years before he accepted God's forgiveness for himself. He was an ordained minister for thirteen years, preaching the gospel to countless people, before he believed in the message himself.

His friend, Peter Böhler, told him, "Preach faith until you have it." One evening a few months later he let the message of forgiveness penetrate his soul. In his journal he describes the experience:

> In the evening I went very unwillingly to a society in Aldersgate Street, where one was reading Luther's preface to the Epistle to the Romans. About a quarter before nine, while he was describing the change which God works in the heart through faith in Christ, I felt my heart strangely warmed. I felt I did trust in Christ, Christ alone, for salvation; and an assurance was given me, that he had taken away *my* sins, even *mine,* and saved me from the law of sin and death.[4]

Like Wesley, it may take us years to receive the message of God's complete forgiveness. We may need to hear it over and over, to teach it and even preach it, before we can make it our own. Once we do, we can expect that our heart, too, will be "strangely warmed."

Confession as a Means of Grace

"So, what about confession and repentance?" people sometimes ask me. "Aren't those still necessary in order to obtain forgiveness?"

I do not believe that they are necessary in order to secure forgiveness, but they are necessary if we are to *experience* forgiveness. The only thing that can provide forgiveness is the sacrificial death of Christ. Nothing else will bring us forgiveness.

As the eloquent preacher of our era Charles Stanley writes, "The basis of our forgiveness is not confession, repentance, or faith, though all three are essential to our experience of forgiveness. The basis of our forgiveness is the sacrificial, substitutionary death of Jesus Christ on the cross."[5]

Through confession I do not obtain forgiveness, but through confession I acknowledge that I have failed, and in doing so I open a channel of communication with God so that I can be changed. When we fall, the important thing is not getting the slate cleaned, nor getting rid of our guilt. The important thing is dealing with the cause of the sin in the first place.

Knowing that God longs to forgive me allows me to turn to God and agree with him that the sinful act was wrong, and then, because I am free to commune with him, begin a discussion about why I committed the act. Now I can say, "God, that was stupid, and I am sorry. I am grateful that you have forgiven me. Thank you. Now, teach me about my heart, show me what is inside, reveal to me what led me to do it. Let's deal with the cause."

Confession is a means of grace. It is a privilege, not a duty. Confession is an activity whereby we invite God to begin working on what has been destroying us. It is not so much an attempt to rid ourselves of the past as it is a way by which we live in union with God. When we find ourselves focusing not so much on our sin but on God himself, we will have arrived.

Forgiven to Focus on Life

I can remember riding my bike as a kid. Whenever I rode over a certain narrow bridge I was afraid that I would veer off the edge. While I was riding I would look at the edge and, invariably, steer myself straight into the creek. One day I decided to quit looking at the pitfalls and keep my eyes focused on the path. I rode right down the bridge and safely to the other side.

The process of receiving God's forgiveness and living in that freedom is the same. When I was focused on *not* failing I invariably failed. I tried hard not to fall, but since falling was what I was thinking about, falling is what I did. Once I began to experience God's forgiveness I quit looking at sin and started looking at God.

I shared the message of God's forgiveness with a bright and committed group of college students from Berkeley and Stanford. At first they resisted the notion of God's complete forgiveness, but during the second day, one by one, I could see some of them beginning to understand and accept God's offer.

During the sharing time at the end, one young man stood up and said, "I was beginning to lose my love for God. I secretly hated God, and I was sick of being a Christian. Now I am excited again. I see now that I was in bondage to something God had already dealt with." Then he added, with a California flair, "Now I am free to live radically for Jesus." That is precisely what God wants us to do.

God offers us forgiveness on his terms, with nothing for us to do except receive it. This enables us to concentrate on the life Jesus came to bring us. We do not need to look to the left or to the right, but instead, we can fix our eyes upon Jesus, who is the author and perfecter of our faith (Heb. 12:2).

Forgiven to Work on the Cause of Sin

When our son, Jacob, was nearly two years old, he had a remarkable vocabulary and a keen sense of how to use words to order his world. When he would do something wrong, like throw his cup across the room, my wife, Meghan, or I would ask him to pick it up. Then we would say, "And what do you say, Jake?" to which he would reply, "I am sorry." We were pleased that he was developing such good manners.

Then one day I noticed the downside of his confession. As soon as he could walk, Jacob was fascinated with the electrical outlets in our home. We told him repeatedly not to put his fingers near the plug. He knew it was wrong, and one night he laughed while he did it. He turned to me and said, "I am sorry, Daddy." He was not sorry. He did it again. Finally, after the third time, I said, "Jacob, it is nice that you say you are sorry, but what I most want you to do is to *stop doing it.*"

The moment I said those words it hit me: God wants to deal with sin itself, not simply get it erased. Once we have sinned it is over; nothing can change what has happened, no matter how bad we feel. What is important is that we work on what caused the sin so that we do not do it again. How sad God must be when he hears us say, "I am sorry," but then we fail to let him heal us.

We are forgiven long before we repent. Experiencing that forgiveness, however, requires that we repent. Because I have been forgiven, because I have been accepted, because God loves me, I am free to walk in holiness. Repentance does not mean that we make some resolution to be morally perfect by tomorrow. Resolutions are mostly a matter of willpower, and they seldom have a positive, lasting effect. I have found that is better to pray than to make resolutions. In our prayers we can let God examine us. Like the psalmist we can pray,

Search me, O God, and know my heart; test me and know my thoughts. See if there is any wicked way in me, and lead me in the way everlasting (Ps. 139:23–24).

Forgiven to Reorder Our Lives

Our forgiveness was obtained at a high price. We must never belittle sin, nor should we think of our forgiveness as a casual cleansing of the slate. It is, as Evelyn Underhill notes, "a stern and painful process" that will require "the reordering of the soul's disordered love."[6] God has forgiven us because he wants to establish a relationship with us. Within that relationship we are enabled to grow, to be healed, and to become whole.

The pain that we have caused through our sin is sometimes staggering and shocking. For years we may have run from God, afraid of his judgment and certain punishment. Off in the distance God stands alone, with a heart broken because we fail to accept his offer of forgiveness. He loves us with a furious passion. He forgives us even when we cannot forgive ourselves. Sometimes I can only sit and wonder at the thought of how much God loves us.

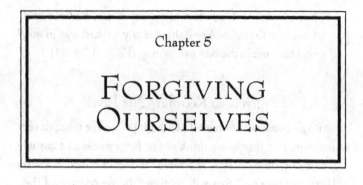

Chapter 5

FORGIVING OURSELVES

I think that if God forgives us we must forgive ourselves.
Otherwise it is almost like setting up ourselves
as a higher tribunal than Him.

C. S. LEWIS

During a time of prayer and confession with a trusted friend I shared a deep and painful sin I had committed as a young man. My friend placed his hands on my head and prayed for me to be go back in my memory to the actual moment of the event, to see the faces and the surroundings, making the past contemporary in the present moment.

When I was able to see the scene in my mind he instructed me to step outside of the event and just observe. I watched myself. Suddenly, I felt my hand clutching on to something. It was the hand of Jesus, who was right there with me. Jesus and I simply gazed at . . . me. Suddenly I was looking at . . . myself. I looked deeply into my own eyes and I felt compassion.

I wanted to give myself a hug. So I approached and embraced myself. In that very moment I was reconciled with myself. I did not overlook or excuse the sin, but I pardoned the sinner, and the sinner was me. God had enabled me to treat myself and my sin exactly as he does—with reconciliation and forgiveness.

Even though I had experienced God's forgiveness for what I had done, I had not forgiven myself until that moment. It is sometimes easier to accept God's forgiveness for things we have done because God is a forgiving God. What is often more difficult is forgiving ourselves for what we have done.

Forgiveness for the Things We Have Done

When my brother, Mike, was seven years old, he told my parents he did not want to go to school anymore. He begged and pleaded with them to let him stay home. My dad tried to persuade him to go to school, but it did not work. Finally, Dad threatened to spank him, and when Mike still refused to go to school, Dad took off the belt and gave him a spanking.

It turned out that Mike did not want to go to school because his first-grade teacher was punishing him with a ruler each time he made a mistake. This teacher was humiliating him, and he cowered in fear. When Dad found out why Mike wanted to stay home, he broke down and cried, and asked Mike to forgive him.

I'd never heard this story until one day not long ago when I asked my dad if there was anything in his long life of seventy years that he regretted. He said there was really only one thing, and that was this incident. Even though this happened over thirty years ago, as my dad told me this story he began to cry.

There are so many things for which we have trouble forgiving ourselves. Reckless things we did as teenagers may still haunt us; cruel things we have said or done to others may still follow us; sexual encounters in our past may still carry pain. I have listened to people share their pain over having had an abortion, their anguish at having left a spouse unfairly, their incredible regret for having harmed someone while driving drunk. These kinds of memories can linger and destroy our ability to go on living with any kind of joy.

When we are unable to forgive ourselves we are forced to live under a dark cloud of remorse. Feelings of self-hatred take residence in our souls and begin to color our whole outlook on life. A deep sense of despair pervades all that we think and do. We sentence ourselves to a lifetime of self-loathing.

Why It Is Difficult to Forgive Ourselves

The reason it is so difficult to forgive ourselves is that it takes courage. It takes fortitude to face our past and ask that it not affect our future. I think of Peter and how guilty he must have felt in abandoning Jesus on the night when Jesus needed him most. He denied Jesus not once, but three times. He would have to live with what he did on that Thursday night for the rest of his life.

When Jesus rose from the dead and appeared to two of his disciples he told them to go and tell the others—especially Peter—that he was alive again, and that he wanted to meet with them. Jesus knew that Peter, more than any other, would feel unwelcome. When Jesus asked Peter three times, "Do you love me?" he was restoring him, healing his memory of the three times he had denied Jesus.

Casting Out the Unforgiving Inquisitor

It is also difficult to forgive ourselves because there lurks within us a voice that condemns us. We will have to come face to face with this demanding judge and abolish its voice from our midst. This will not be easy, and in fact, it will require divine assistance. As Lewis Smedes, a professor at Fuller Theological Seminary, notes, "It takes a miracle of love to get rid of the unforgiving inquisitor lurking in the shadows of your heart."[1]

I believe that this is one of the great tools of the devil. The enemy of our souls will try to play back the tapes of our past whenever he thinks we need a strong dose of guilt. These tapes may have been played back so many times that we have memorized every detail. Learning how to shut off the tape is not easy, but it is something we can learn to do.

Forgiving ourselves can be made doubly difficult if there are people in our lives who do not want us to be free of our past. These people usually have a judge of their own, and they have been hounded by that voice for years. Hearing that you have forgiven yourself for a past sin will make them angry. Misery does indeed love company. It will take courage on our part to deny their voices as well and claim a forgiveness that is rightly ours.

Parting with Guilt

Another reason it is difficult to forgive ourselves is that we may have surrendered ourselves to the guilt we feel and grown comfortable with it. Even though it is destroying us, it is familiar, and we are sometimes more comfortable with what we know than with what we don't know. The prospect of waking up tomorrow without guilt is so foreign that we may choose to hold on to our shame. It may be depressing, but at least it is safe.

I will never forget something a friend of mine said when he, thanks to good counseling and the correction of a chemical imbalance, was beginning to come out of a long life of depression: "I don't know how to live these days. I lived so long with my guilt that I feel strange without it. I grew accustomed to living every day in pain, and it is hard to let go of it."

Even though the longing of our hearts is to part with our pain, there is something in us that desires the familiar. The longer we have defined ourselves by our past, the more difficult it will be to let go of the guilt. If we have grown accustomed to seeing the world in black and white, it will take some adjusting to get used to a world full of color again.

Banishing the Fear of Future Failure

A final reason it is difficult to forgive ourselves is the fear of future failure. Because of what we have done in the past we assume that we will do the same in the future. If we forgive ourselves, we reason, we will only make matters worse. By keeping ourselves in the prison of condemnation we hope to keep our behavior in check.

This is really a fear of freedom. To claim our forgiveness is to be free of what we have done. When we forgive ourselves we are proclaiming that we have been emancipated from our past. If we venture into the land of freedom, we suspect that it will be a short stay. Sooner or later we will sin again, and we will be forced to return to our cell. Why not save some time and just keep on condemning ourselves?

The fear of future failure is a lie that paralyzes us. Just because we did something in our past does not mean that we will do it in the future. There is no real reason to expect that we will repeat our past behavior, but by focusing on it we will increase the likelihood that we will. At some point we will have to confront this lie and proclaim its opposing truth: what we have done in no way must determine what we will do. If we can claim our freedom from these lies, we will be ready to begin the work of forgiving ourselves.

Why We Can Forgive Ourselves

The first thing we must establish is the grounds for forgiving ourselves. The basis upon which we dare forgive ourselves is the fact that God has forgiven us. God's love, manifest in forgiving us, is the foundation upon which we can begin the process of forgiving ourselves. Because God, who sees all and knows all, has declared us forgiven, it is only natural that we would go on to forgive ourselves.

It is the cross of Jesus that has established our forgiveness. We can confront our past only with the solid fact of

God's forgiveness. In his compassion God has cast our sins into the sea (Micah 7:19), removed them from us as far as the east is from the west (Psalm 103:12), and remembers them no more (Jer. 31:34). This is how God has chosen to deal with our past, enabling us to do the same.

Seeing from God's Perspective

One of the greatest obstacles to forgiving ourselves is our tendency to view forgiveness as something *we* do. Charles Stanley calls this "performance based forgiveness."[2] Our entire society is built upon a performance system wherein we receive in proportion to our performance. If we have done well, we are applauded; if we fail, we are rejected.

We transfer this same mentality into the area of forgiveness. It is common for us to place a value on our past mistake: a white lie is a small sin, adultery is a large sin. If we follow this system, a small sin would require only a small price, such as feeling mildly guilty, but a large sin would demand a much higher penalty, such as spending a lifetime of regret.

God does not view our actions in the same way we do. God does not measure sin, or place a greater or lesser value on certain sins. Jesus forgave an adulterous woman (John 8:3–11) in the same manner he forgave the paralytic (Mark 2:5). God does not make distinctions between our sins; he does not weigh them against one another or forgive them partially. God forgives any and every sin.

Our struggle is not about being forgiven, it is about *feeling* forgiven. Because we are so accustomed to a performance-based approach to forgiveness, it is difficult to feel forgiven for the more damaging mistakes of the past. It is easier for most of us to forgive ourselves for a minor infraction, such as feeling anger toward someone, than it is to forgive ourselves for a major violation, such as killing someone. God, however, sees them identically (Matt. 5:21–22). More importantly for us, God forgives them identically. This is the perspective we must have if we are going to forgive ourselves as God forgives us.

Seeing Ourselves as We Are

The final part of the foundation is learning to see ourselves as we truly are. We need to develop a proper identity if we are to forgive ourselves. In today's world, we are prone to viewing ourselves primarily as righteous people who are capable of doing sinful things, as opposed to being sinful people who are capable of doing righteous things. The difference in perspective is monumental.

If I see myself as a righteous person, I expect very little failure. Doing good is what comes naturally to a good person. God, too, I reason, must expect a lot of success from me. Failure, sin, and error occur only when I lose focus, only when I am lazy. If I work hard enough, I can live flawlessly. God is not particularly pleased when I do something good, some act of kindness or courage, because that is what he expected in the first place.

But if I see myself as a weak and broken person, I am not shocked by failure. It does not throw me out of kilter. I certainly do not hope for it, expect it, or easily excuse it, but I am not startled by it. Failure, sin, and error do not happen because I get lazy; they are a part of being a fallen person in a fallen world. God is not shocked by my sin; he knows that I am dust (Psalm 103:14). When I do something courageous, or self-sacrificing, God is pleased. Given all that is against me, a kind act is a thing of awe in God's eyes.

God expects more failure from us than we do from ourselves because God knows who we are. We are not the righteous person who occasionally sins, we are the sinful person who occasionally—by God's grace—gets it right. When we start from this perspective we are released from the bondage of perfectionism and are able to forgive ourselves once and for all. We are to take our cue from him. We may be disappointed with ourselves, but God is not. We may feel like condemning ourselves, but God does not.

What does God do? God brings our actions to the light, calls them what they are, gently reminds us *who* we are and *whose* we are, and helps us *believe* that we have been forgiven so we can be *reconciled* with ourselves. God then allows us to *celebrate* his kindness, and in the future, *remember* the event from a new perspective. Honesty, identity, faith, reconciliation, celebration, and redemptive remembering: These are the names of the six stages we encounter in the process of forgiving ourselves. The sins we have committed need not determine our future, but rather, a right reaction to them can chart the course of our destiny to a land of freedom.

Honesty

The first stage involves being honest. I notice I have a tendency to deceive myself, to rationalize my behavior, or to look for a scapegoat. I do this because I have a hard time admitting failure. I learned quite early that I could shade the truth just enough to avoid recrimination. "Oh, you see, I was, uh, really going through a hard time . . . "

At some point we will have to quit rationalizing and simply say, "I did it. I am to blame." When it comes to forgiving ourselves we must first tell the truth, the whole truth, and nothing but the truth. George Buttrick, a Presbyterian pastor, encourages people to be very specific when making a confession. He believes we must "set hooks into facts" if we are to find forgiveness.[3] As long as we are uncertain about what we have done we will remain uncertain about our forgiveness. Once we are able to name the exact event for which we want to find forgiveness, the work has begun.

Identity

The second stage involves acknowledging who we are. One of the reasons confession is so difficult is that it destroys our pride. When we confess we are admitting that we are not perfect. The masks come off and we reveal our true selves. This is not easy to do, but it is an essential step toward forgiving ourselves.

We are more foolish than we would like to admit. We are weak and faulty. When we take ownership of this we are able to be honest with ourselves and with others. Knowing who we are frees us from the need to appear as something we are not. Once we do we are on the path of self-forgiveness.

God's power is made perfect in our weakness (2 Cor. 12:9). Humility unlocks the door of forgiveness. At some point we will have to look upon ourselves with compassion and abandon the need to expect perfection. Knowing who we are helps us to be tender toward ourselves.

Faith

The third stage involves an act of faith. God has forgiven us. It is one thing to hear that and another to receive it. We can never forgive ourselves by our own efforts. Only when we rely on the faith and work of Jesus do we have the right to forgive ourselves.

In one of his prayers Kierkegaard wrote:

> If I try to cover myself against the guilt of sin and the wrath of heaven, I will be driven to madness and despair. But if I *rely* on you to cover my sins, I shall find peace and joy. You suffered and died on the cross to shelter us from our guilt, and take upon yourself the wrath that we deserve. Let me *rest* under you, and may you transform me into your likeness. [4]

Kierkegaard knew that he could not forgive himself; trying to do so would drive him to madness and despair. Notice the two words he uses to describe his part in the transaction of forgiveness: *rely* and *rest*. Those are verbs of faith.

Relying on what God, through Jesus, has done for us, and resting in that promise, is our only hope. We need to be gentle with ourselves and acknowledge our unbelief. God knows how much or how little we believe, and the only thing God desires is that we increasingly trust in his forgiveness.

Faith is risky and daring, but it is not unreasonable. We need not grasp it overnight. We can take small steps, such as reading the Bible's account of forgiveness, soaking it in, memorizing passages, becoming familiar with what it says. We can also pray for faith. It is a gift God loves to give. As we are able to believe in the forgiveness God has established, we will be able to forgive ourselves.

Reconciliation

The fourth stage involves making peace. At some point we will have to reconcile with the person we have been so angry with: ourselves. In the opening story of this chapter I told how I needed to "hug" myself. That was a yearning for reconciliation. I had been so angry at myself for so many years that I had become an enemy to my own self. When I saw myself with the compassionate eyes of God, I wanted to restore all of the years I had wasted in self-hatred.

We have been given the opportunity to make peace with ourselves. There is no reason to wait. The person we have been so disappointed with, the person we have learned to hate for what that person did, is standing in front of us. Reconciliation becomes possible when we take a risk and say, "I forgive you. I am sorry I have spent all of this time trying to hurt you. All of that is over now. I forgive you."

Celebration

Jesus forgave many people, and with few exceptions, these people all rejoiced and celebrated their freedom. Mary Magdalene, Zaccheus, Matthew, Peter—all of them were found out and forgiven. Jesus said when a soul is reconciled to God the angels rejoice: "I tell you, there is joy in the presence of the angels of God over one sinner who repents" (Luke 15:10). If the angels are celebrating, shouldn't we?

Celebrations help us acknowledge the goodness of God. They provide visible, concrete reminders of what God has done for us, and they allow us to revel in it. God became one of us because he loves us: let us feast and call it Christmas. God died and rose in order to save us: let us rejoice and call it Easter. God loves it when we celebrate his goodness.

I am suggesting that we consecrate and confirm our reconciliation with a celebration of reckless gratitude. Why not have a party? What about a feast? Perhaps we could take time out and spend a day in solitude simply basking in the gift of forgiveness.

One time I celebrated my forgiveness by pretending I had just been released from prison ("the Penitentiary of Condemnation"). I decided to spend the day as if I had been returned to society, and I looked upon the time as a new beginning. I even bought myself a new pair of shoes. I was now walking in freedom.

Redemptive Remembering

The Bible declares that God remembers our sin no more (Jer. 31:34). I am not certain as to what that means. God, being God, could certainly do anything, even forget something, despite being all-knowing. If we take Jeremiah literally, then we can say that God actually chooses to forget our sins. What I am certain about is this: God treats me exactly as if he did not remember. God never brings up past sins, and he regards me as if they had never happened at all.

We are not capable of forgetting. The memory of a difficult event will always be with us. But we can choose to remember in a redemptive manner.[5] We can remember the event as a time of real pain but also as a testimony of God's forgiveness and grace. We will always remember our mistakes, but we can also remember that they led to healing.

Once we have passed through the stages of honesty, identity, faith, and reconciliation, we will begin living our lives free of the past, but that past still remains. When we are confronted with what we have done, we can now say, "Yes, that did happen, but it has been forgiven, and now stands as a witness to the love of God." In this way we redeem even the memory of our pain.

Forgiving for Not Forgiving

Because forgiving ourselves is not an easy task, it will take time, and we will likely continue to wrestle with the old voices of condemnation. Perhaps you are at a place in your life where it seems impossible to forgive yourself. The first thing you can do is forgive yourself for not forgiving yourself.

We are not God. When God forgives he does so swiftly and without question. When we forgive ourselves we do so slowly and with great misgiving. The wounds of our sins may still be fresh, and it will take time for us even to begin seeing them properly. In this case, we should forgive as far as we can, and pray that we stay on the task.

This work of forgiving ourselves begins in our mind and descends into our heart. We may have a mental understanding of God's forgiveness, and we may actually believe in it intellectually. But the truth may not have reached the depths of our soul. We might know in our head that we have been forgiven, but it has not reached our heart. Even still, God is gracious toward us.

Rewriting the Script of Our Lives

If we have truly forgiven ourselves, we will begin living life anew. One of the blessings we will discover is that forgiving ourselves allows us to define ourselves as God does, and not according to the sins we have committed. Paul admonished the Corinthians to give up drunkenness and fornication by telling them, "This is what some of you *used to be*. But you were washed, you were sanctified, you were justified in the name of the Lord Jesus Christ and in the Spirit of our God" (1 Cor. 6:11). And so for us, no longer must we define ourselves by our past actions, but rather, we are defined by who we are in Christ.

"When you forgive yourself," writes Lewis Smedes, "you re-write your script. What you are in your present scene is not tied down to what you did in an earlier scene. The bad guy you played in Act One is eliminated and you play Act Two as a good guy."[6]

I think this is why I am drawn to plays and movies in which a character goes through a transformation. I do not like movies that are supposed to depict "real life" stories where the characters go through no change for good, where in the end no one is a hero and everyone remains in despair. I like to see characters move beyond their past failures because I want that for myself.

Forgiving ourselves is a step toward transformation. We are not forced to be who we were; we are now free to be who God wants us to be. We can look at our past sins and know that they cannot determine our present, except as a means of making us more aware of our need for God's grace.

When we experience God's forgiveness we draw closer to God. We have been treated with mercy, and we cannot look to God except in gratitude. The transaction of forgiveness helps us to be more dependent upon God and more wary of ourselves. In this sense, and only this, our past evil can be transformed into something good.

Forgiven to Forgive

It is difficult to know exactly when we have forgiven ourselves. For some it will be instantaneous, like a flash, and suddenly the guilt of the past has disappeared. This is rare; in most cases we will not know when it has happened. If there is any sign that we have actually forgiven ourselves, it is this: We can love freely.

When forgiveness has taken root inside of us we can see it in our willingness to withhold judgment toward others. We know that we have forgiven ourselves when we are able to forgive the wrongs that others have done to us. God has graciously forgiven us, and if we no longer hold ourselves in contempt, how can we not forgive others? Freely we have been forgiven, freely we now forgive.

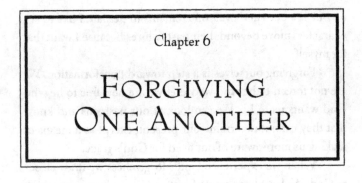

Chapter 6

FORGIVING
ONE ANOTHER

Let us go to Calvary to learn how we may be forgiven.
And let us linger there to learn how to forgive.

C. H. SPURGEON

Roger Frederikson is a tender and compassionate pastor who for over forty years has healed broken hearts and mended hurting churches. He recently shared a story with me about how God healed his own heart in a surprising way. Not long ago he was reading a book about how we sometimes live with the pain of not forgiving without even knowing it. He was discussing the book with his wife when she said, "I think you have some unfinished business to take care of."

Her prophetic words led Roger to listen to his heart. Through prayer he realized there was, in fact, someone he had not forgiven. Many years back his younger brother, whom he loved very much, was killed in an automobile accident. Roger was thirty-seven years old, and his brother, who was twenty, had gone for a drive with some of his friends. They began to drive a little recklessly, and the driver lost control of the car. When the car crashed only one of the six passengers was killed: Roger's brother.

Though the driver of the car attended the funeral, he never spoke to anyone, nor did he ever call to apologize to their mother. This was what hurt Roger the most. He never spoke to the man after that incident, and for over thirty years carried a secret anger in his heart, unknown even to himself. After his time of prayer he knew what the "unfinished business" was all about: he felt he needed to find that man and forgive him.

He searched and searched and could not track him down. Finally, after some time, he came upon a phone number and dialed it. The man's wife answered and he asked to speak to him, but she said that he had died four months before. Roger's heart sank.

He decided to share with the man's wife why he was calling, and during the course of their conversation Roger began to feel a mending in his heart. Even though the man was no longer with them in body, Roger said to her, "Please promise me that you will find a way to tell him that I forgive him." She promised that she would. They cried together, and through their tears they found comfort. The unfinished business was now finished. The gift of forgiveness had been given.

The Many Ways We Get Hurt

God invented forgiveness because he knew that we were capable of harming one another, and he knew that forgiveness was the only way to heal our broken hearts. Our lives are full of the hurt caused by other people. Unkind words, broken promises, physical abuse, violence, neglect, and malice toward one another are a part of our broken world.

We get hurt, and the hurt is real. I have listened to frightening stories of rape and physical abuse that have made me wonder why God even created human beings. I have experienced the pain and anguish of being hurt, sometimes physically, and sometimes verbally.

One day while I was driving home, a man who was drunk tried to run me down. He pulled alongside of me and tried to force me to pull over. When I finally did he came over and pulled me out of my car and started screaming at me, claiming that I had cut him off. With my hands at my side I began to say that I did not remember cutting him off, but that if I did I was sorry. Before I could say the word "sorry" he punched me in the face so hard that blood spilled all over the road. He hit me two more times, and would have hit me more, but someone watching called the police, so he sped away.

Sometimes the harm done to us is verbal. Words are powerful weapons that can do great damage. I remember one time a person made a vicious statement about me, a totally unfounded lie that was a cheap attempt to slander my character. I walked around for several days with a sick feeling, as if someone had kicked me in the stomach. I wanted vengeance! I wished that my accuser could have seen how much pain I was experiencing, all because of a few words.

And sometimes it is not what someone does but what they don't do that hurts us. Words of encouragement or love that go unspoken; times together between a parent and child that never occur. Children who are given up for adoption may feel abandoned. A father who walks out on his family leaves a lasting pain. The ways in which we hurt one another are myriad. In situations like these Jesus' encouragement that we forgive one another seems like an impossible task.

Why It Is Difficult to Forgive

When we have been hurt—really hurt—forgiveness is very difficult. In fact, forgiving the one who hurt us is the last thing we want to do. As C. S. Lewis said, "Everyone says forgiveness is a lovely idea, until they have something to forgive."[1] We want to see our offender punished, we yearn to see justice served, and we long for the day when the person who hurt us crawls at our feet and begs us to forgive them.

Forgiving is difficult because it seems unjust. If a person has truly harmed us, it is only right that they pay for their crime. It appears to be an unjust acquittal to forgive someone before they have paid their debt for having harmed us. Forgiveness does not make sense to us; retribution seems warranted.

It is difficult to forgive because we long for justice. Forgiveness is not about *justice*, it is about *healing*. It is not logical, and it is not fair. But it is the way to real freedom, and if we can navigate through the turbulent waters of our pain and ask God's help in forgiving those we need to forgive, we will experience an inner peace that this world does not understand.

Misconceptions About Forgiveness

There are four misconceptions about forgiveness that need to be addressed because they are responsible for preventing many of us from embarking on this journey of healing. First, there is the misconception that to forgive is to condone the behavior. If we forgive someone, we assume we are judging them to be innocent. This is simply bad logic. Forgiving someone does not imply that we deem their actions as acceptable; in fact, we judge what they have done as absolutely unacceptable.

We have to separate the offender from the offense. As G. K. Chesterton observed, "Christianity . . . divided the crime from the criminal. The criminal we must forgive unto seventy times seven. The crime we must not forgive at all."[2] The action must never be excused. Forgiveness is not about condoning or excusing or overlooking the offense.

A second misconception about forgiving someone is that it is only necessary when it actually changes the one who harmed us. We assume that as long as that person remains unrepentant, as long as that person does not ask for forgiveness, to forgive them would be futile. But forgiveness is not a reforming act, it is a releasing act. We do not forgive someone in order to change them. We forgive in order to set ourselves free.

A third misconception that keeps many of us from forgiving is the cliché "Time heals all wounds." Time never healed any spiritual wounds. If this were true, then why is it that people can live for many years still hurting from something done to them in the distant past? Roger's story at the beginning of this chapter shows us how it is possible to live with the same pain for thirty years. Time does not heal wounds; only God heals our wounds.

A fourth misconception is that to forgive means that we also must forget. When we forgive someone we are not pretending that an offense never happened. To "forgive and forget" is not only impossible but dangerous. Far too many people spend a lifetime trying to forget things only to find out that you cannot bury the past, it can only be dealt with. Try as we may, it will remain with us.

The Pain We Suffer in Not Forgiving

If forgiveness does not mean reform on the part of the one who hurt us, and if it does not mean restoration for the damage that has been done, then *why should we forgive?* Because experience has taught that the *failure to forgive damages us*. We enslave ourselves to the past when we refuse to forgive, letting what has happened in the past determine our future. We may think that by not forgiving someone we are getting even, but in reality we are the ones who lose.

The attitude "God may forgive you, but I never will" may seem like we are enacting some form of justice. We may think we are holding that person accountable, but all we are really doing is continuing to hold on to the pain. In not forgiving we actually increase the pain of the past by letting it accumulate interest. Each day the anguish carries forward, doing more damage than the actual incident itself.

The attempt to get even by not forgiving destroys us in the long run. The hate and anger we feel surges in us like a white-hot passion, but in time it saps us of our strength and prevents us from moving on. The longer we harbor the resentment, the deeper the scars we develop.

I met a woman who had been angry at her mother for as long as she could remember. Each time she mentioned her mother she began to shake with anger. Her mother had always laid unfair expectations on her, and she believed she was inferior her whole life. Sometime in her midthirties she realized she was clutching the pain of the past, and that it was only doing her harm. When she was finally able to forgive her mother, she said, "I wish I had done that years ago."

Setting the Prisoner Free

The only way we can be healed of the things that have hurt us is to forgive. This is why Jesus was so insistent upon it. He knew that an unwillingness to forgive only prolongs *our own* agony. When you forgive a person, writes Lewis Smedes, "you set a prisoner free, but you discover that the real prisoner was yourself."[3]

When we have decided to set the prisoners free, to put the pain of the past behind us, we will embark on a healing journey that typically involves four elements: discovering how much you have been forgiven, releasing the person of the debt they owe, accepting the person as they are, and allowing God to turn the evil into good.[4] Each one is essential to our spiritual health, so it is important that we take a closer look at them.

The Healing Journey

In order to see and feel what the healing journey of forgiveness is like, I want to share the story of my friend Stan. I first met Stan when he came to my office looking for someone—anyone—to help him settle down. He was visibly shaken, unable to look me in the eye. His voice quavered as he told me he had attempted suicide the night before. After a brief discussion, I called a Christian counselor, who for the next six months helped him find stability.

A year later he wandered into a church where I was preaching on the subject of God's love, acceptance, and complete forgiveness. He came by my office later that day and asked how a person could experience that, and after an hour's discussion he said he was ready to accept God's acceptance of him. In his prayer Stan asked God to begin working in his life.

His spiritual life was like the ascent of a rocket—quick and powerful and wonderful to watch. He was changing each day as he began to realize how much God loved him. He likened himself to a "caterpillar who had become a butterfly." Then came the day I was not expecting. During one of our discussions he told me that when he was a young boy he was molested by a friend of the family. The hurt and harm done to him was tremendous; his entire adolescence was spent in self-hatred. In fact, his attempted suicide was the culmination of his agony.

But now everything was different, he said. He could look at his past with different eyes, the kind of eyes God has when he looks at us. He told me that it was hard to forgive himself, that for years he thought *he* was responsible, but now all of the condemnation had melted away. The process of Stan's healing simply amazed me.

Then one day, about six months later, he said, "I have a question. I have been thinking about how God has done so much for me, and forgiven me for so much, and I was wondering if you thought it would be okay if I forgave the man who hurt me?"

I stammered for a moment. My own anger toward that man (whom I had never met) was still alive in me. "Well, I suppose that, if you feel it is right, you should do that, Stan." He went to the man and shared about his faith in God, and he said to him, "I just want you to know that I forgive you for what you did to me."

Even more, he went on to tell him that God wanted to forgive him as well, and that God loved him and wanted him to be happy. The man wanted to know more about Stan's faith, and they talked for hours about God's offer of forgiveness. Stan was able to turn his painful past into a hopeful future, and he has helped others do the same. Stories like these are staggering to our sense of justice, but in God's economy of forgiveness the only injustice is not to forgive.

Knowing Our Own Forgiveness

Stan's story provides us with a beautiful picture of forgiveness. In it we can see the elements that are a part of forgiving someone who has hurt us. The first thing that his story shows us is that a clear sense of the forgiveness of God will lead us to

forgive one another. Paul told the Ephesians, "forgive one another *as Christ has forgiven you*" (Eph. 4:23). Paul appealed to
the forgiveness of God as the ground for forgiving one another.

When Jesus told his disciples to pray "forgive us as we
forgive," he was not giving them a *prescription* for forgiveness
but a *description* of what those who have been forgiven *do*. It is
a statement about reality: I forgive exactly as I have been forgiven. It is an undeniable fact that if I am not forgiving, I do
not understand how much I have been forgiven.

We are called to forgive one another because God has
forgiven us. Paul exhorted the Colossians, "Bear with one another and, if anyone has a complaint against another, forgive
each other; just as the Lord has forgiven you, so you also must
forgive" (Col. 3:13). Jesus told his disciples not to come to
God in prayer if there was someone they needed to forgive. It
appears that in God's view forgiveness is more important than
prayer (Mark 11:25).

Stan wanted to forgive the man who abused him because of his own experience of being forgiven. Stan let go of
the need to punish himself, and he experienced a freedom that
filled him with joy. It was so wonderful that he wanted to share
it with everyone—even with the one who had harmed him.

Releasing the Debt

When someone has injured us they have incurred a debt.
They owe us something. That is why it is so hard to forgive
someone who has not made restitution, who has not paid the
debt they owe us. Forgiveness is about releasing a debt that

someone has not paid, and may not ever pay. In fact, the payment is inconsequential. When we forgive we release the debt. We are saying, "There is no longer anything you must do. I am freeing you of this debit, wiping out the deficit."

That is exactly what Stan did when he told the man he had forgiven him. He relinquished the debt. In essence, he was saying to him, "For years I held on to this debt, but it was only ruining me. I wiped it out, and in so doing let us both out of the prison of our past. We are both free of what happened."

Accepting the Offender as They Are

When I am harmed I want to see that person not only brought to justice, but also changed—*before* I will forgive. My hope is that the person will undergo some transformation that will justify my forgiveness. Unfortunately, this may never happen, and I cannot wait for that person to change in order to get on with my life.

When Stan approached this man he was not interested in whether or not the man had changed. This man had done nothing to prompt Stan to forgive him, and in fact, at first he tried to rationalize what had happened. None of this mattered to Stan. He accepted the person as he was, and he demanded no change in order to forgive him.

There are no strings attached to forgiveness. The releasing of the debt requires no future reformation of behavior. If it did, it would not be forgiveness. As long as we hold on to the need to see the person change, we will still be enslaved to the past. We will go free only when we absolve the person completely, and that includes letting them be who they are.

Allowing God to Turn Evil into Good

The final element of forgiveness is allowing God to use what has happened as a means of growth for us. Nothing can change what has happened, but in the providence of God's overarching care for us, even that which is evil can become something good.

While I wish that Stan had never gone through this experience, marvelous things have happened as a result of it. First, it was instrumental in leading him to God's acceptance and love. It also helped him be more sensitive and sympathetic to people who have been through similar struggles. Finally, his story is a great example of the power of God to transform lives.

God can take something harmful and painful and use it to make something more beautiful—like the story of Joseph, whose brothers, out of jealousy, faked his death and then sold him into slavery, though he later rose to incredible heights. Joseph said to his brothers, "Even though you intended to do harm to me, *God intended it for good*" (Gen. 50:20). Joseph would later feed and care for the brothers who once did something evil to him.

Though I do not believe that God would ever send us evil, he can use our suffering as a means of spiritual growth. Once when I was truly harmed by the unkind words of a friend, I was reluctant to forgive him for several years. During a time of prayer I sensed the burden of my unforgiving spirit, so I asked God what to do. "Forgive him," God said.

"How?" I asked.

"Imagine that he is sitting in the chair across from you. Talk to him, and tell him you forgive him," the Voice whispered.

I did so, and immediately felt like a weight was lifted off of me. I thought it was over, but God suddenly urged me to consider how damaging words can be. We began a discussion about the words I use, about how careless I can be when speaking about someone who is not present. What was once just a painful experience became a tool in my own growth.

Forgiving When It Is Difficult to Forgive

The two most difficult people to forgive are those whom we cannot forgive because they are no longer with us and those who simply do not care whether or not we forgive them.

When Roger heard that the driver of the car had died, he was disappointed because he felt he had missed the chance to forgive him. If he had gone to visit him a year earlier, he would have been able to speak the words "I forgive you" face to face. While Roger would have preferred that, his story reveals to us that a person need not be alive in order for us to forgive him or her. He came away from that phone call feeling as if the forgiveness was complete, even if the man was not physically present.

Forgiving those who do not want our forgiveness is difficult because there is something inside of us that wants them to desire our forgiveness. Forgiving is a very hard thing to do; we do not do it casually. So when we actually forgive someone we want them to receive it with gratitude. However, their failure to want our forgiveness does not need to prevent us from forgiving them. It is not our offender's desire to be forgiven that has prompted us to forgive, it is our desire to be free. Their attitude should not dictate our behavior.

Completing the Transaction of Forgiveness

We have talked a lot about the role and response of the offended, but what about the offender? So far that person has done nothing in the process. As I have said, it is possible—even necessary—for us to forgive someone even if they do not know we have forgiven them and even if they do not care.

Ideally, however, the transaction of forgiveness is fully realized by having a face to face meeting with the one who harmed us. In some cases it is unwise to approach the person face to face. Some people will react negatively to our forgiveness, or perhaps they will try to justify what happened.

While it is not necessary to forgive someone in person, it may be the best course of action. We should try to do so under two circumstances: one, when the person has asked for forgiveness, and two, when we have a *very clear sense* that it is the right thing to do. It should never be done impetuously, but, through prayer and through the guidance of those whom we trust, we should be able to discern when it would help.

If we do feel that it would be good to confront the one who harmed us, we would do well to keep this in mind: the issue is not about right and wrong, the issue is about releasing the debt. I once confronted someone who had injured me and found myself wanting to show them how wrong and how foolish they had been. Instead of forgiving them, I actually tried to make them feel worse than they already did. I realized I was not ready to forgive that person.

We need to take time and be sure that we are really ready to forgive or we run the risk of creating a deeper hurt. We are ready when we discover that our desire to meet with the person is not to condemn but to set both prisoners free.

We Know We Have Forgiven When . . .

Much like forgiving ourselves, forgiving others will take time, and sometimes we will not know the exact moment when we have actually forgiven someone. There are, however, two indicators that let us know we are on the high road to freedom.

One indication that we have forgiven is when the old, dark, angry feelings surrounding the event have dissipated. We might have a slight emotional response when we think about it, but by and large we are unmoved. Memories that once made us sick or furious now pass through our mind with little attention. If the thought of the person or the event still sends us into an emotional frenzy, we may still need more time to work on forgiving.

Another indication that we have forgiven is that we actually find ourselves wishing the person well. While in seminary I was assaulted and mugged by four young men after coming home from class. They kidnapped me at gunpoint, but later released me. I was basically unharmed, but it was a frightening experience. They were caught later that same night and sent to jail, not only for what they did to me but for several other crimes as well.

A few years later I prayed that God would help me forgive them. Then one day I found myself thinking about them, wondering how their lives had turned out. I tried to contact them, but the police would not let me have their names or know their whereabouts. Nonetheless, I began praying for them, wishing them well, and asking God to help them know about his love and forgiveness. Suddenly, I realized that I had truly forgiven them.

Love Covers a Multitude of Sins

For years I understood the phrase "love covers a multitude of sins" (1 Pet. 4:8) to mean that by loving others I could cover up *my* sins. Because I had many sins, I thought I had better try to love a lot! Then one day it hit me: love for one another leads us to cover *their* sins. When I am immersed in God's love and acceptance and forgiveness I am drawn to forgive the sins of the people around me. I lose my desire for revenge and find myself longing to show mercy.

Forgiveness is a gift God has given us to wipe away the sins of others, not only for their sakes but for our benefit as well. Forgiving one another sets us free from the stifling grip of an unforgiving spirit. The prisoners walk free, the evil is transformed into good, the pain stops, and life is ours to enjoy again. God is indeed a loving God.

PART THREE

EXPERIENCING GOD'S CARE

Chapter 7

GOD'S CARE

The Kingdom is the serenity of God already enfolding us.

EVELYN UNDERHILL

George Muller was dedicated to the cause of helping those in need. He founded an orphan ministry that struggled to survive. At one point Muller wrote concerning this ministry, "The funds are exhausted. We have been reduced so low as to be at the point of selling those things which could be spared." Muller and his co-workers prayed for the next four days, when suddenly a woman arrived at their door, bringing with her sufficient funds for the orphanage. She told them she had been traveling for four days.

Muller made the following observation: "That the money had been so near the orphan house for several days without being given, is a plain proof that *it was from the beginning in the heart of God to help us.*"[1] Muller's whole life was an ongoing testimony to the care of God. With each passing day he learned to trust God more and more as he was able to see God's invisible hand at work.

One day he was telling a man that the Bristol orphanage was having some difficulties providing enough food for the orphans. When he finished the man said, "You seem to live from hand to mouth." "Yes," said Muller, "it is my mouth, but it is God's hand."[2] Muller lived his entire life believing that God not only desires to care for us but, in fact, does so each and every day.

Does God Really Care?

Many of us live with a tremendous amount of worry, anxiety, and fear. Life is difficult, and we have learned to be defensive, to protect ourselves. Perhaps we have faced a tragedy or a crisis and felt that God was not with us. We hear stories, like the ones about George Muller, and wonder, "Does God really cares for us, or are these events simply coincidences?" If God is really loving, then how can we be sure? If God really cares for us, then why do we still suffer?

The problem is that God chooses to remain anonymous when he cares for us. In the story of George Muller's orphanage, we will never know if the woman came as an answer to their prayers or if she simply came out of human kindness. We will never know because God's tender love for us is not coercive. If God had dropped the money from the sky, then it would have taken away the possibility of doubt, and thereby taken away Mr. Muller's ability to believe freely. God, in his love, always leaves room for us to doubt. But God also gives plenty of reason to believe.

Life Without God

One day I asked myself, "If there were no God, what would life be like?" I tried to imagine how I would feel, and I wrote down the words that came to mind: anxious, worried, afraid, hopeless. If there were no God, this world would be even more frightening than it already is.

Even though I believe that God cares for us, I still wrestle with my faith when I see people living in poverty, struggling to stay alive, or suffering from the pain of loneliness. I begin to doubt God's care when I hear stories about mothers who murder their own children, or when I see footage of bloodshed, violence, and war. My soul cries out, "Where are you, God?!!!"

I am learning that God values our freedom so much that he does not violate it, even to alleviate our suffering. I am also learning that God is very present in our pain, and in fact, is more present in our times of suffering than at any other time in our lives. A man who works with mentally and physically handicapped people said that he asks himself this question at the end of each day: "How did I experience the presence of Jesus in the pain of someone today?"

And I have also abandoned the glib notion that all those who believe in God will experience perfect peace and prosperity. Life is difficult, no matter how much faith you have. But in the midst of it there is a Spirit of comfort that cannot be destroyed. At times God allows us to feel empty and afraid, confused and uncertain, but he never abandons us.

Be Still and Know

My wife, Meghan, and I were so excited when we found out she was pregnant that we told everyone we knew. We called all of our relatives and friends, who shared in our joy. I was beginning to imagine what the baby would look like, wondering if it was a boy or a girl. It was the greatest feeling of exhilaration and joy either of us had ever felt.

Four days later she began to bleed, and we feared that she might be having a miscarriage. Sitting anxiously in the doctor's office waiting for the result of the tests, I paced and trembled and prayed that God would come to our rescue. But when the doctor returned, he said Meghan had indeed had a miscarriage. Suddenly the whole world collapsed around us.

A lot of people tried to console us by saying things like, "It'll be okay, you'll have another child," but none of it seemed to help. I tried to be strong for Meghan, and she tried to be strong for me, but we were living in a cloud of despair. A few weeks later I was praying with a friend when a woman I barely knew stopped by for a visit. As far as I know, she did not know about the miscarriage. She came into the room, looked me straight in the eyes, and said, "Be still and know that he is God." Her gentle voice spoke with a kind of authority that conveyed the power of God.

I left with a strange feeling inside of me. I could not get that verse out of my head: "Be still, and know that I am God"

(Ps. 46:10). After a few hours a feeling of warmth and comfort came over me. I realized that God was in control, that even though I could not make sense of it, God could. I was given a sense of peace, an assurance that all would be well, even if I could not understand it.

Three months later we found out Meghan was pregnant again. When she told me, the very first thing I did was to pray. God whispered into my heart, "Do not be afraid. All will be well." Those words continued to resonate inside of me, not only that day, but for the next nine months. A sense of peace presided over any anxiety I might have.

It is natural to panic during a crisis, to run hurriedly, think rapidly, and act irrationally. It is in those moments that we are to be still, because it is only when we are still that we can hear that gentle voice saying over and over, "I am God, I am God, I am God." The voice reminds us that *we* are not God, and that is a very good thing, indeed.

Do Not Be Afraid

Of all the words God has spoken to me over the years, "Do not be afraid" have to be the most frequent. I know that it is God when I hear those words in the depths of my soul. Perfect love casts out fear (1 John 4:18), so I have come to recognize that it is God who is speaking when those words calm me down.

I usually fear something in my life. Planes, trains, and automobiles seem to crash all around us. People I know and love get sick and die. Friends get divorced. Children are abused. It is a dark and frightening world. "Do not be afraid" echoes in my soul. Though fear frequently overtakes me, I am usually not afraid for long. I know that God is in control. Even if I should make a mess of things, even if something terrible occurs, I know that God is able to accomplish his ends.

God will never forget me. Like a mother whose child is nursing at her breast, God could never forget me. Even if a mother could forget, God will never forget (Isa. 49:15). The compassionate care of God is the foundation of my trust. I am not trusting in myself, nor in my government, to protect me; I am learning to trust God, and therefore I am at peace.

What Is God Like?

We often find it difficult to trust God because we know so little about God, for he is greater than we can imagine and too vast for us to comprehend. That is why Jesus is so important to us. Jesus provides for us the clearest picture of the nature of God. We see in Jesus the compassion of God, the tenderness of God, and the desire of God to care for us. Even if we had never heard his words but simply watched his actions, we would know something of the character of God.

One day I decided to go through the gospel of Mark in one sitting. With a highlighter in hand, I underlined every verb used to describe the actions of Jesus. When I was finished I found that this exercise had taught me more about the nature of God than anything I had ever done.

The first verb Mark used to describe Jesus' action is "came." Jesus *came* to be with us. God's first move is to be among us—Immanuel, God is with us. God comes to us long before we come to God. We may think we are in pursuit of

God, but in reality we are only responding to a God who has been pursuing us.

There is more. Mark tells of a Jesus who "taught," "cured," "took her by the hand and lifted her up," and "forgave." We see a Jesus who "sat at dinner," "had compassion," and "laid hands" on people. He "blessed," he "sang," he "cried out," he "died," and he "rose from the dead." These are verbs of compassion. If we want to know what God is like, all we have to do is look at what Jesus did.

The Promises of God

In addition to looking at what he did, we can also learn about God's care for us by listening to what he said. Jesus left us with promises that are solid and unchanging. There are two that my own experience has tested and found true. The first is this: "So I say to you, Ask, and it will be given you; search, and you will find; knock, and the door will be opened for you" (Luke 11:9).

Jesus promised us that God would respond to our needs. If we come to God in faith, we will not be turned away. When we ask we *will* receive, but the answer may not come as we thought it would. God is too gracious to answer all of our prayers. In looking back over the years I have noticed that many of my prayers were often misguided and misinformed. I am thankful that God does not answer every prayer as I have prayed it.

Martin Luther said that we should never prescribe measure, manner, time, or place in our prayers because he believed that we should trust in God's wisdom, which is higher than ours. Jesus said something similar when he told his disciples, "When you are praying, do not heap up empty phrases as the Gentiles do; for they think that they will be heard because of their many words. Do not be like them, for *your Father knows what you need before you ask him"* (Matt. 6:7–8). God looks in our heart and sees what we really need. The answer may not come as we anticipate, but I have learned that it will come.

I keep a prayer journal, writing down each person or situation I am praying for, as well as the request I make to God. Each of them is dated, so I know exactly when I began praying for some situation. When I look back over the journal I am stunned by three things: one, God eventually answers all my prayers; two, the answers rarely resemble my requests; and three, the answers are always better. It is an exercise that has taught me to trust in God's wisdom.

I am often reminded of a prayer that is believed to have been written by a Confederate soldier during the Civil War. This prayer reveals how higher blessings often come in ways we did not seek them:

> I asked for strength
>> *that I might achieve;*
> I was made weak
>> *that I might learn humbly to obey.*
> I asked for health
>> *that I might do greater things;*
> I was given infirmity
>> *that I might do better things.*

I asked for riches
that I might be happy;
I was given poverty
that I might be wise.
I asked for power
that I might have the praise of men;
I was given weakness
that I might feel the need of God.
I asked for all things
that I might enjoy life;
I was given life
that I might enjoy all things.
I got nothing that I had asked for—
but everything that I had hoped for.
Almost despite myself,
my unspoken prayers were answered;
I am . . . most richly blessed.[3]

I Will Never Leave You

The second promise I have come to rely on is this: "I will never leave you or forsake you" (Heb. 13:5). One of the most significant people in my journey is a person I met only once. At the age of eighty-four, he was a man of deep and gentle wisdom. I asked him what was the most important truth he had learned in his long life. He said, "God has never left me. I have suffered a lot, but God was always with me. That is not only the most important truth I have learned, it is really the *only* thing I really believe to be true."

I have never forgotten that conversation. My own life confirms what he said. I have experienced times of great doubt, I have been angry at God, and I have even had times when I felt like God had abandoned me, but when I look back I see that God was there all along. No matter what we do, God will never leave us.

The apostle Paul faced times of trial and persecution, but he always felt the presence of Christ. He wrote, "We are afflicted in every way, but not crushed; perplexed, but not driven to despair; persecuted, but not forsaken; struck down, but not destroyed; always carrying in the body the death of Jesus, so that the life of Jesus may also be made visible in our bodies" (2 Cor. 4:8–10). He believed that his own sufferings, far from leading him to doubt God's presence, actually increased his awareness of Christ's life within him.

The Secret of the Blessed Life

God is with us. This is the secret of the blessed life. The kind of existence described in the Twenty-third Psalm is available to all of us. "The LORD is my shepherd, I shall not want" (Ps. 23:1), writes the psalmist. The Hebrew phrase is literally rendered, "I lack nothing." The psalmist could make this bold statement because he believed that God's presence is all that we need in life. Because God is with us we can lie down in peace, find sustenance for our soul, and even walk through death's dark valley with courage.

The Bible is full of stories of God being *with* people. Enoch walked *with* God for three hundred years (Gen. 5:22); God was *with* Ishmael when he was alone in the wilderness

(Gen. 21:20); Jacob was promised by God, "Know that I am *with* you and will keep you wherever you go" (Gen. 28:15); and God promised to help Moses overcome his fear of speaking to Pharaoh, saying, "Now go, and I will be *with* your mouth and teach you what you are to speak" (Exod. 4:12).

Finally, Jesus told his followers, "And remember, I am *with* you always, to the end of the age" (Matt. 28:20). It is the promise of God's presence that makes us able to say with the author of Hebrews, "The Lord is my helper; I will not be afraid. What can anyone do to me?" (Heb. 13:6). We will never face a situation without the presence and care of God.

Free from Anxiety

Because God was always with him, Paul would often say, "Do not worry about anything" (Phil. 4:6). Anxiety is the great sickness in our society. Paul's words seem like an impossible command for most of us, who do well not to worry about *everything*. The looming national debt, the sputtering economy, the presence of guns in our schools, the spread of AIDS, and the rapidly changing job market create a people who are frightened and anxious about the future.

The only reason Paul was able to tell the Philippians not to worry was because he knew that God was alive and present and caring for them. He finishes the verse by saying, "but in everything by *prayer* and supplication with thanksgiving let your requests be made known to God." Do not worry, Paul says, but instead turn to God in prayer.

Peter did the same when he said, "Cast all your anxiety on him, because he cares for you" (1 Pet. 5:7). God actually wants us to bring our cares to him. It is God's design that we take whatever is bothering us, whatever concerns we have, whatever needs we would like to see filled, to him in prayer.

Several years ago a friend taught me how to "bundle" my concerns in a package and give them to God. I refer to them as "care" packages because they are full of my cares. When I pray I find it helpful to write down all of the things I am anxious about: meeting deadlines, friends who are in trouble, loved ones who are hurting, and so on. When I have compiled the list I turn to God and say, "I have a present for you. Here are all of my concerns. I give them to you gladly, and I know that you are able to care for them in ways far better than I can."

God loves these kinds of packages. Prayer was God's invention. The care and compassion God has for us is greater than we could ever imagine. We often think that God is too busy to bother with such a trifling concern as a friend's lost job or home. How untrue! God cares about what we care about, even if it seems trivial.

Of Stars and Tires

Wendell Barnett is a pastor in Oregon who is always letting God use him to care for others. He recently told me the story of a man he knew who was in need of a new set of tires but did not have the money for them. The man prayed that God might help him find a way, but he was reluctant to ask anyone for help. Wendell also noticed that the man's car needed new tires, but didn't want to interfere in his business without being asked, so he, too, decided to pray about the situation. Soon after, an old friend of Wendell's called him and said he had a pair of brand new tires he did not need and wondered if Wendell knew anyone who might need them. He said he did, and to Wendell's amazement, they fit the man's car exactly.

Tires? Is God interested in tires? Doesn't God have something better to do than go around finding people tires? Apparently not. From God's point of view there is nothing more wonderful than caring for our needs. For most of us, the real task is coming to believe that God really desires to provide for our needs.

It is nothing for God to do such a thing. For people like Wendell, who are always looking and listening, these things happen all of the time. God is infinite in wisdom, strength, and power. God could make a few thousand stars and answer a "tire" prayer without much effort. God could, but is God willing?

Most of us have difficulty believing that God really cares for us. We have trouble believing that God is always present, always gracious, and always providing for our needs. Like the psalmist we ask, "When I look at your heavens, the work of your fingers, the moon and the stars that you have established; *what are human beings that you are mindful of them, mortals that you care for them?*" (Ps. 8:3–4).

Surely God must be busy with things like the troubles in the Middle East, or the poverty in Bangladesh, or the destruction of the environment. Our small troubles—and even some of our big ones—seem inconsequential. We think that our "care" packages, like letters to Santa, are sent but never opened.

The Bible describes a God who is so in love with us that he never leaves us. According to Psalm 139, there is no place we can go where God is not. If we go to the top of the mountain, God is there; if we go to the deepest valley, God is there; if we descend even into hell itself, God would follow us there.

If God is concerned about making the grass green, and about feeding the birds, who are here today and gone tomorrow, how much more is God concerned about you? (Matt. 6:30). There is no cry that goes unheard; the ears of God hear them all. God grieves with us, and rejoices with us. He hears the deepest yearnings of our hearts, even those we cannot hear ourselves. Even though God can make a new solar system with a single word, it seems that he enjoys giving good gifts to his children, even a set of tires.

Peace, Not as the World Gives

When Jesus told his disciples that he would be leaving, they were understandably afraid. But he tried to reassure them, saying, "Peace I leave with you; my peace I give to you. I do not give to you as the world gives. Do not let your hearts be troubled, and do not let them be afraid" (John 14:27).

The peace that the world gives comes through strength and wealth, through security alarms and world treaties, through safe neighborhood watches and dual air bags. The peace the world gives is fleeting and unstable. The peace that Jesus offered comes from the fact that he will never leave us or forsake us (Heb. 13:5).

Peace is not the absence of strife but the presence of Christ. No matter what we face, we face it with the power and presence of one who has overcome the world. For he said, "I have said this to you, so that in me you may have peace. In the world you face persecution. But take courage; I have conquered the world!" (John 16:33).

Isaacs and Ishmaels

Sometimes, despite our best intentions, we fail to let God provide for us, and instead we assume control of our destiny. When Abraham and Sarah were promised to be the parents of many nations they assumed that they would have children right away. When Sarah did not get pregnant for many years, they began to doubt God and tried to find a solution of their own. They decided that Abraham should try to have a child with their servant, Hagar. Soon after, Hagar got pregnant and gave birth to a son, Ishmael.

It was not until they were in their nineties that God fulfilled the original promise, as Sarah gave birth to Isaac. God gave them a promise, but in between the *promise* and the *provision* they had to be *patient*. Many of us know what this is like. God has said that he will care for us, but when we run into a problem we may be tempted to create an Ishmael.

God promises that he will provide for us, but that promise often comes with a challenge. This is not because God wants to be cruel but because he wants us to grow. Waiting for the provision takes a great deal of faith, patience, and trust. God molds and shapes our souls through this process. It may seem painful at the time, but it is the only way God can increase our faith.

God answered George Muller's prayer for financial help the moment he prayed for it. He continued to pray over the next four days though the prayer had already been answered.

Muller writes, "God allowed us to pray so long . . . to try our faith, and to make the answer so much sweeter."[4]

St. Patrick's Prayer

Like George Muller, St. Patrick knew firsthand about the providential care and protection of God. He suffered many trials, illnesses, and persecutions, and testified that God carried him through them all. He left us a famous prayer that invokes the power of God to protect, guide, and lead.

> Christ to protect me to-day
>   against poison, against burning,
>   against drowning, against wounding,
>   so that there may come abundance of reward.
> Christ with me, Christ before me, Christ behind me,
> Christ in me, Christ beneath me, Christ above me,
> Christ on my right, Christ on my left,
> Christ where I lie, Christ where I sit, Christ where
>   I arise,
> Christ in the heart of every man who thinks of me,
> Christ in the mouth of every man who speaks of me,
> Christ in every eye that sees me,
> Christ in every ear that hears me.

BREASTPLATE PRAYER OF ST. PATRICK[5]

The Widespread Mercy

In the grand scheme of life there is much to be thankful for. George Buttrick tells the story about a man who stood in front of a group of people and held up a large piece of white paper with a single black blot in the middle of the page. He asked everyone what they saw, and they all responded, "a blot." Not a single person said, "a white piece of paper." Buttrick concludes, "There is an ingratitude in human nature by which we notice the black disfigurement and forget the widespread mercy."[6]

Buttrick then encourages his readers to write down all of the things for which they are grateful. I did this exercise and found what he said to be true: I could start, but I could never stop. I began to thank God for caring for me by providing things like the air we breathe, the sun that lights our day, and the rain that falls and makes things green. God's love, I realized, is in the laughter we hear, and it is in the things that make us smile: a rootbeer float, a cartoon, a festive parade, a fond memory.

God's care for us is far greater than we can imagine. God has given us all of these things because he wants us to enjoy our lives. Under God's watchful, loving, embracing, attentive care, we are now able to care for ourselves as God cares for us.

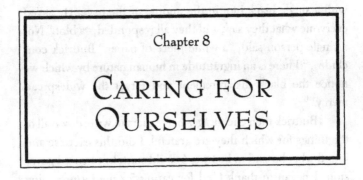

Chapter 8

CARING FOR OURSELVES

*What if you discovered that the least of the brethren of Jesus,
the one who needs your love the most, the one you can help
the most by loving, the one to whom your love will be most
meaningful—what if you discovered that this least of
the brethren of Jesus . . . is you?*

CARL JUNG

A couple of years ago I began to feel fatigued. At the end of every week I would come home and collapse for a few hours, but then immediately feel the pressure to catch up on some project I had been putting off. Meghan began to notice how tired I was, and she said, "You need to slow down." I never dreamed of taking time off to relax because there were too many things I felt needed to be done, and I was sure *I* was the one to do them.

Each Monday morning I began what seemed like an endless race to accomplish as much as I could. I sensed that I needed to rest, but like many of us, I simply pushed those thoughts out of my head and forged on. I knew that I had overextended myself the evening I came home and was so exhausted I did not even have the strength to play with Jacob. "I am sorry, Jake, Daddy needs to rest for a while." I collapsed on the couch.

A few days later I came across an article on the fourth commandment: "Remember the Sabbath and keep it holy" (Exod. 20:8). In the midst of the hurry and hustle I sensed that keeping the Sabbath was something I needed to learn about, so I read an entire book on the subject of the Sabbath. I shared some of the ideas with Meghan, and at first she was not sure about them, but she became interested when I explained that keeping the Sabbath would allow us to spend more uninterrupted time together as a family.

Over the next few months we discovered what Jesus meant when he said, "The Sabbath was made for humankind, and not humankind for the Sabbath" (Mark 2:27). We learned why God commands it, what it is, and what it is not. As soon as we started keeping the Sabbath we noticed a change in our family, our relationships, our jobs, and our spiritual lives.

Meghan began to come up with great ideas, such as putting a day's worth of meals in the crock pot on Saturday night so that we could eat from it all day on Sunday. We made Sunday a day of complete rest from the chores of life. No trips, no travel, no yard work; just leisure and conversation and board games and walks in the park. Our rule of thumb was this: we can do almost anything as long as it *accomplishes nothing*. It may sound strange, but this was extremely difficult to do. It also had a dramatic effect on our lives.

The really staggering thing I discovered is that God cares about how we care for ourselves. For a long time I thought it was selfish to care for oneself, that one needed to suffer and deprive oneself of any comfort or joy. In instituting the Sabbath God shows that he cares for us by insisting that we rest our bodies and give space to our souls one day a week. Coming to understand this freed me to begin discovering what it meant to care for ourselves.

Allowing God to Care for Us

Caring for ourselves is largely a matter of allowing God to care for us. Part of the way God cares for us is to hide from us. Because God values our freedom and will not coerce us into loving him or being obedient to him, God remains present but invisible to us. If we are to become aware of God's presence, we must search. This searching, this intentional openness to God's presence, is the primary way we care for ourselves.

I have come to realize that a lot of our religious behavior is actually designed to keep God at a distance. That is why it is so crucial for us to find ways to invite God's presence into our lives. Keeping the Sabbath was, for Meghan and me, a great way to create space to allow God to enter into our everyday existence. We cared for ourselves by allowing God's life and love to penetrate our home.

God invites us to integrate his presence, his resources, his wisdom, and his power into our lives. We are invited to go through our day and watch this happen. God wills that we solicit his help in every aspect of our lives, particularly those that we find difficult. God suffers when he sees us try to work through strained relationships, painful memories, and family trials on our own. Caring for ourselves as God would have us do will mean allowing God to be a part of our lives.

All that is required on our part is to believe and to seek. "I keep the LORD always before me; because he is at my right hand, I shall not be moved" (Ps. 16:8), wrote David. He made an effort to keep his attention fixed on the presence of God. God is here. God is present, even now as you read. Our conscious awareness is often focused on something else, so that we do not live with any kind of awareness of the presence of God. David knew that by *keeping God before him* he was being strengthened, so much so that he could say, "I shall not be moved." The foundation of caring for ourselves is the fact that God is with us.

Why We Are Here

Why is God with us? Why are we even here? We are here because God is preparing us to be something so special that through all of the ages we will be the primary testimony of his love. Our life is about what God is making us. Human life, from God's perspective, is meant to be dramatic and exciting. We were built to be God-inhabited, created to live on bread that this world knows nothing of.

Each of us came into this world for a single purpose: to glorify God and enjoy him forever.[1] We were uniquely created, each different and distinct from one another, but we were all created so that one day we would stand before the heavenly host as an eternal trophy of God's goodness, grace, and tender mercy.

We did not make ourselves. Our existence is not due to anything we have done. God has created us out of love, and through his ongoing presence and desire to be among us, he intends that each one of us would stand as a witness to that love. We were created because we were loved, we were created so that we could experience that love, and we were created so that we could become a symbol of that love.

Who We Are

Who are we, that God should love us so much? We are magnificent creatures, fearfully and wonderfully made beings, with massive souls comprised of eternal matter that will far outlive the bodies we inhabit.

Who we are, and what we are made of, has always been a mystery. The Bible speaks of us as having a soul, a spirit, and a body. Paul wrote to the Thessalonian Christians, "May the God of peace himself sanctify you entirely; and may your *spirit* and *soul* and *body* be kept sound and blameless at the coming of our Lord Jesus Christ" (1 Thess. 5:23). Caring for ourselves involves nurturing and sustaining all three of these aspects of who we are. We are spiritual beings, we have souls, and we inhabit bodies. God created all three and placed us in charge of their care.

Caring for Our Spirits

For many years I did not understand the importance of the resurrection of Jesus. I knew that the cross was God's way of forgiving our sins, but the resurrection remained a mystery. It was not until years later I discovered that the resurrection was more than Jesus' greatest miracle, it was *God's means of imparting new life* to our dead spirits.

When Jesus rose from the dead he conquered death and made his life—eternal life—available to any and all who would receive him.

The very life of Christ was given so that we might be made alive together with him. When we are baptized we are united with Jesus in his death and in his resurrection (Rom. 6:3–4). A new life is born, a new self emerges—the true self we were meant to be.

We were created to contain this new life within us. The Bible refers to it as being "born from above" (John 3:3, 7). This new birth requires nurture and care. If we are to grow toward maturity, we will need to pay attention to this life we have been given. The new self, the true self, that we are in Christ requires ongoing spiritual sustenance. This is why God has left us certain exercises and activities that allow spiritual life and power to flow through us.

Prayer, for example, is a spiritual exercise. It is a means of receiving God's grace, a channel through which we receive the life and power of God. Memorizing and meditating on the Bible, taking the sacraments, and fasting are also spiritual exercises that fortify this life within us. For centuries the saints have attested to the power made available to us through the practice of certain spiritual disciplines. Caring for our new self involves engaging in these activities on a regular basis as a way of nurturing the life of Christ within us.

Caring for Our Souls

By their very nature, our souls defy definition. There is no way to quantify or even describe them with accuracy. The soul is the part of us that feels and enjoys, yearns and weeps, desires and wills. Our souls are comprised of our emotions, our passions, and our feelings. This aspect of who we are needs attention and care, but all too often we neglect it. Contemporary psychologist and theologian Thomas Moore writes,

> The great malady of the twentieth century, implicated in all of our troubles and affecting us individually and socially, is "loss of soul." When soul is neglected, it doesn't just go away; it appears symptomatically in obsessions, addictions, violence, and loss of meaning."[2]

When our souls are not cared for they will find ways to let us know. Some of the pain we experience comes from the fact that we have neglected our emotions, refused to pay attention to our feelings, and denied our God-given passions.

The first thing we can do is to become sensitive to this dimension of who we are. "Taking an interest in one's own soul," Moore goes on to say, "requires a certain amount of space for reflection and appreciation."[3] Creating space in our lives will mean finding time for relaxation and enjoyment, time when we simply gaze at the wonder of creation, moments of quiet reflection.

Soul care involves living close to our hearts, not at odds with them. We must pay attention to what we feel. Much of the time I monitor and judge my feelings before I get a chance to experience them. "You shouldn't feel that way," I tell myself the moment anxiety, fear, or depression emerges. But I *do* feel that way. The feeling may not reflect the entire truth of a situation, but it is true for me, and it should not be suppressed.

Caring for our souls has a lot to do with being who we are, and letting things be as they are. My soul rebels when I try to manipulate and control my world as opposed to experiencing and enjoying what life brings. My soul longs to be set free, to wonder, to imagine, and to savor the world. I am even learning to appreciate my times of sadness, which is also a way to care for my soul.

Our souls are worth trusting. When we allow ourselves to experience healthy pleasure, to enjoy the world around us, we are caring for our souls. I love baseball, for example. There is nothing particularly spiritual about watching baseball, but I enjoy it. I even enjoy poring over box scores the day after a game. This may seem like a waste of time, especially to someone who doesn't like baseball, but to me it is a way to enjoy life, a way to care for my soul.

Others find joy in music, poetry, or a good novel, in bird-watching, astronomy, or needlepoint. I believe God encourages us to enjoy whatever gives us pleasure. He gave us a soul so that we might reflect on the wonder of our existence, and also that we might appreciate who we are and all that we have been given.

Caring for Our Bodies

Our souls and spirits are housed in our bodies. In this life we will never exist apart from them. God has chosen for us to be embodied, and because of that, we are to love and nurture and be thankful for the bodies we have been given. We may not like them, or we may wish that they looked differently than they do, but they are, nonetheless, miraculous creations.

We are comprised of bones and blood and muscles and cells and organs, all put together in such a way that both the scientist and the poet marvel. The working of the human eye alone is enough to make us dizzy with wonder. In a flash it can focus on an image and transfer it to the brain, so quickly that we can recognize the face of an old friend in an instant.

Why do we have bodies? Why did God make us with bodies? Our bodies are the primary receptacles for the life of God. "Do you not know" wrote St. Paul, "that your body is a temple of the Holy Spirit within you, which you have from God, and that you are not your own?" (1 Cor. 6:19). The spiritual life and the bodily life are not opposed to each other, and in fact, they are inseparable.

The body was designed for interaction with the spiritual realm through the disciplines of the spiritual life.[4] Everything that we do, we do in our bodies; everything we do with our bodies affects our souls and our spirits. This is an important point for us to learn, and one we easily miss. In one section of C. S. Lewis's *The Screwtape Letters,* the senior devil tells the junior devil to try and persuade the Christian whom he is tempting to believe that the body is inconsequential:

> At the very least, they can be persuaded that the bodily position makes no difference to their prayers; for they constantly forget, what you must always remember, that they are animals and that *whatever their bodies do affects their souls.*[5]

Because our souls are affected by what we do with our bodies, it is crucial that we care for them.

We care for our bodies by treating them well: eating healthy food, exercising, getting plenty of rest. Our bodies are to be respected and monitored, not despised. If we take proper care of them, they will reward us with energy and vitality, they will allow us to experience more and more of the grandeur of life, they will enable us to extend the power of God to others.

A few years ago I realized that my life was almost devoid of any exercise or play, but I did not think there was anything spiritually dangerous about this. Then one day I was praying and I said, "I need direction, Lord. I feel like something is missing. Can you tell me what I need to do?" After a long silence I heard one word: play. Over the course of the next fifteen minutes I talked with God about this, and I was given a strong sense that I needed to go out and just have fun, to be outdoors, and to play.

One of the first things I did was to plant a garden. It only yielded a few dozen tomatoes, but it did great things for my soul. It was St. Pachomius who noted, "The place in the monastery which is closest to God is not the church, but the garden. There the monks are at their happiest."[6] God loves to see us happy, playful, and enjoying his creation. God has placed us in charge of these wonderful bodies, and in caring for them we are caring for a beloved part of his creation.

Spiritual Formation

The body was designed to interact with the spiritual realm. When we engage in certain spiritual exercises (all of which involve our bodies) we nurture and develop our souls and spirits. This process is called *spiritual formation*. Sometimes when we hear a term like spiritual formation we think, "This is too hard for me. This is not practical. I don't think that I can I do it in my own life."

Spiritual formation is something that is happening all of the time, regardless of whether or not we are aware of it. Each moment that passes forms our spirits. Our soul, said sixteenth-century reformer Johann Arndt, is like wax. Whatever we impress upon it, it holds that image. Therefore, he writes, "your soul will show the image of that to which you turn it."[7] Each day our spirits are being formed. The question is, Are they being formed into the image of God?

If we "turn" ourselves, as Arndt put it, to God, we will begin to reflect God in our everyday lives. This is not only the goal of Christian spiritual formation, it is the highest way we can care for ourselves. This turning means engaging in activities that enable God to become more involved in our lives.

There are many spiritual exercises that can draw us closer to God, but the six that have had the greatest effect on me are Sabbath-keeping, solitude, silence, prayer, study, and practicing the presence of God. Some of them involve withdrawal or abstinence, and some of them require active engagement or attentive focus. All of them are a means of God's grace, divinely appointed activities that turn us to heaven so that we might reflect its glory.

Exercises of Abstinence

We care for ourselves not only by what we do but also in what we refrain from doing: working, being with people, and speaking. Keeping a Sabbath, entering into solitude, and enjoying the freedom of silence are three essential ways we can care for ourselves. By withdrawing from work, people, and words, we allow God to make us whole.

As I mentioned above, learning to observe the *Sabbath* is a blessing. We are often so accustomed to pushing ourselves beyond what our bodies, souls, and spirits can bear that we need times of withdrawal from any kind of work. One day a week, or for an afternoon or two, we should schedule a time in which we do absolutely nothing. Abstaining from any kind of work is sometimes the hardest thing to do, but it teaches us to live in trust. As modern writer Marva Dawn notes, "A great benefit of Sabbath keeping is that we learn to let God take care of us—not by becoming passive and lazy, but in the freedom of giving up our feeble attempts to be God in our own lives."[8]

Another spiritual discipline that has greatly benefited my soul is *solitude*. In this activity we withdraw from other people for the purpose of becoming more attuned to our inner heart. Solitude also makes us more sensitive to the world around us. It creates a space wherein we can come to "the still point of the turning world."[9] My soul longs for these kinds of spaces, even if it is only for a brief period. Occasionally I will stop what I am doing and go to a quiet place to be alone. I come away refreshed and more attuned to those around me.

At other times I will engage in the discipline of *silence* as a means of centering my spirit and quieting my soul. We live in a culture that hurls words at us through television, radio, and newspapers. Words have become cheapened in our day. Silence allows us to recover the value and the power of words. By keeping a period of silence we become more focused on the things that we say without words, the things we communicate in a smile, a gesture, or our facial expression.

Exercises of Engagement

We also care for ourselves by what we do. What we focus on, and what we set our minds upon, will influence our souls. Prayer, study, and practicing the presence of God are three effective ways we colabor with God in an effort to care for ourselves. By conversing with God, fixing our minds upon truth, and becoming consciously aware of God's presence, we allow God to penetrate our lives.

Prayer is one of the most transforming activities we can engage in. Prayer, according to Richard Foster, is "finding the heart's true home."[10] God has given us the gift of prayer because he wants us to commune with him. Through prayer we take all our needs and concerns, all our questions and doubts, to a God who understands and welcomes them. Many times

I have looked to God in desperation, pleading for a word of encouragement or insight, and God has never failed. The answer has not always come as I wanted it to, or when I wanted it to, but it has always come.

Study is another transforming experience, since what we focus our minds on has a direct effect on our habits and behavior. That is why Paul urged us to think upon those things that are true, honorable, just, and pure (Phil. 4:8). Richard Foster defines study as "a specific kind of experience in which through careful attention to reality the mind is enabled to move in a certain direction."[11]

One of the ways I study is to take one passage of the Bible and memorize it. For the next several days I will "chew" on that verse, reflecting on its meaning, and marveling at the many ways it applies to my life. After a day or two the verse will have become a part of me, the words will have penetrated my soul, and their truth will have set me free (John 8:32).

A final activity that helps me care for my spirit, soul, and body is often referred to as *practicing the presence of God*. This exercise involves becoming consciously aware of God's presence. We are often focused on so many other things that God is far from our minds. By taking time every few hours to consider that God is present, and is ever-present, we open windows for God to be more and more a part of our lives.

Frank Laubach, Brother Lawrence, Thomas Kelly, and Jean-Pierre de Caussade are four people who have written extensively on this practice.[12] They testify to the glorious hours that can be spent when we expand our awareness to include God. In each of these exercises of engagement we are creating more space in our lives for God.

How to Spend One Day Caring for Yourself

What does all of this look like in a normal day, not a special day set aside for prayer or silent retreat, but an average day? How can we go through a typical day caring for ourselves? A good day of caring for my soul, spirit, and body looks something like this:

When I wake up the first thing I do is get my thoughts in order. Before I get out of bed I do two things. First, I say to myself: "By the grace of God I am loved, I am forgiven, and I am cared for." Good soul care involves soaking ourselves in our true identity and getting a view of the day from God's perspective. This helps me get my roots established.

Second, I try to turn my entire life over to God. I say, "Lord, I want you to direct my whole day—all of my thoughts, words, and actions." This allows God to mold and shape me, and it reminds me that I am not in control of my life. My old self cannot remain intact and in control. This act of daily surrender enables God to nourish and care for my soul.

Third, I want to eat meals that are both nourishing and enjoyable. My body will not respond to too many rich, heavy meals, but conversely, my soul will begin to suffer if I eat nothing but bland and boring food. In addition, a good day for my body would also include a time for exercise and play. If it were an especially good day, I might plunge my body into a hot bath.

Fourth, I will want to take time to be quiet and alone as well as to enjoy the company of others. There is too much noise in the world, and it affects the serenity of our souls. However, we also need to be with people because we are social animals as well. Fifteen minutes of solitude and an evening of good conversation with close friends will strengthen my spirit.

Fifth, a good day also includes time set aside for prayer. For fifteen minutes or so I will lift up the needs of people around me, bathing them in prayer. Also, as I go through the day I will make a conscious effort to be aware of the presence of God every few hours or so.

Sixth, I will want to exercise my mind, reading and studying something that is stimulating and moves me to think higher thoughts. I might read through an entire gospel in one sitting, or memorize a passage of the Bible, or I may spend an evening watching a PBS show on nature.

Finally, I will try to get to bed early. Getting enough sleep is an essential part of caring for ourselves. God never intended us to be tired. If we are exhausted, we create a condition in which we will not be able to enjoy our lives. As I fall asleep I will pray, using the Lord's Prayer, or perhaps the Twenty-third Psalm as my guide. I will tell God that I am grateful for the day that has passed, and that I look forward to the day ahead. On a very good day I will fall asleep in prayer.

Adding Life to Our Years

People always talk about how to add years to your life, but seldom do they talk about how to add *life* to your *years*. Life is too short to live it the way many of us do. The following is my "Life is too short to . . . " list.[13]

Life is too short to work a job I do not like, too short to keep the whole house clean all of the time, and too short to spend more than a few nights a week away from home. It's too short to read all of the junk mail, too short to eat factory-baked bread, and too short not to take a nap when I need one.

Life is too short to let a day pass without hugging my wife, child, and friends, too short to wear neckties every day, and too short to care about whether all of my clothes match. It's too short to stay indoors when the trees turn color in fall, or when it snows, or when the spring blossoms come out.

Life is too short to work in a room without windows, too short to put off telling friends and family that I love them, and too short to live at a distance from people I care about. It's too short to eat rice cakes every day, too short not to run through the sprinklers, and too short not to try something new once a week.

We will never be able to do all of the things we want to do in this life. That is why it is crucial that we spend our time well. Sometimes it takes a serious illness before we learn that life is too short not to care for ourselves. When author Marc Ian Barasch was diagnosed with cancer it changed his outlook dramatically. He writes,

> In the seven years since my cancer operation, I have been living a life that would have once been inconceivable to me. I turn off the phone in the morning, never skip breakfast, occasionally miss deadlines, or even, penury aside, turn down work if it starts to take too much from me, or take me too far from those I love. There is much I still want to accomplish, but my old ambition feels like glorified running in place. My career, which I had fixed on as an unassailable virtue, now seems like a bit of a con. "Wherever you go, there you are." Where did I think I was going?[14]

It is all too easy to neglect our lives, these precious gifts over which God has put us in charge. Our spirits, our souls, and our bodies are some of God's most beautiful creations. We honor him by caring for ourselves.

Caring for Self Through Relationships

"No man is an island," wrote the pastor and poet John Donne. We are all intertwined with one another, and our lives were meant to be lived in community with and for one another. If we are to care for ourselves as God cares for us, we will find ourselves caring not only for our own spirits, souls, and bodies but for those of everyone around us.

"There is no way toward divine love except through the discovery of human intimacy and community," writes Thomas Moore. "One feeds the other."[15] God's love for us has been manifest in the form of tender care, and that care is received by us as we engage in a lifestyle that creates space for God to interact with us. The movement of that divine love will, by necessity, begin to flow out from us and into the lives of those around us. The love of God is made manifest in the love we receive and give to others. The more we are able to give, both to ourselves and to one another, the more we are able to receive.

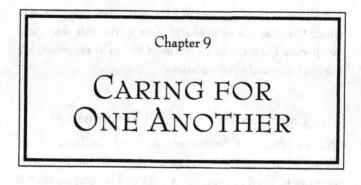

Chapter 9

CARING FOR ONE ANOTHER

I am convinced that nine out of every ten persons seeing a psychiatrist do not need one. They need somebody who will love them with God's love . . . and they will get well.

PAUL TOURNIER

One evening I was invited to a communion service with a small group of about twenty men and women. I had not known these people for very long, and I felt a little out of place. It was a very informal and relaxed gathering. We sat around a large table, lit only by candles. No one had been designated as a leader, so we all took turns sharing anything that was on our hearts. At first I was very reluctant to participate because it was so unstructured, which made me feel uncomfortable.

We sang some familiar hymns and praise choruses, followed by a time of silent prayer. A few minutes later someone read from the Scriptures, and then began to teach a little on the meaning of the passage. After she finished teaching, people began to share some of their own hurts and needs, and each person was received with warmth and encouragement. Then we took part in what was one of the most beautiful communion services I had ever experienced.

As the bread came into my hands I actually felt the presence of Christ. I looked around the room and saw that everyone was holding a piece of bread from the same loaf, that each of us was holding the body of Christ. A woman began to pray, "Brothers and sisters . . . " I didn't hear the rest of her prayer. I looked around at all of the bowed heads and it struck me, "These people are my *family*. That woman is my sister, that man is my brother."

For the rest of the evening I felt a kinship with every person in the room. It was like the meal shared by the two people on the road to Emmaus: in the breaking of the bread I saw the presence of Christ in our midst. We were held together by the love God had shown each of us; that was our common bond. When I walked to my car that night I felt as if I had just seen a glimpse of what heaven might be.

It Is Not Good to Be Alone

God has made us interdependent. From the moment of our creation God felt that it was important for us to live in community. He looked at Adam and said, "It is not good that the man should be alone; I will make him a helper as his partner"

(Gen. 2:18). At the core of our being is a need to love and be loved by others. The great wonder of our existence is the fact that God has made us incomplete. Only by living in community can we find the fulfillment for which we hunger.

Our need to love and be loved is an inescapable fact of our existence. God has designed us this way because God values human community. He could have dispensed all of our necessities directly to us, so that we would have had no need of each other. Instead, he gives us all of the resources we need to care for one another and encourages us to share those resources.

The Vast Network of Care

We live in a vast network of care in which each of us has been given precious offerings from God and is called to pass on these gifts to those who need them. I am fascinated by the story of Joseph Baly, a man who wrote several books that courageously address suffering and death. Mr. Baly knew about grief firsthand: he buried three sons—an eighteen-day-old infant, a five year old who had leukemia, and an eighteen year old who had hemophilia complications after a sledding accident.

His oldest son had been engaged to a young woman before his death, and after he died she was concerned for Joseph Baly and his wife. She gave them a poem that had given her much encouragement. The poem was written by Dietrich Bonhoeffer, a German pastor, who wrote it for his fiancée just three months before he was executed in prison. Bonhoeffer's fiancée later had the poem published. In that poem he wrote,

Should it be ours to drain the cup of grieving,
even to the dregs of pain, at thy command,
we will not falter, thankfully receiving
all that is given by thy loving hand.[1]

When Joseph Baly wrote his book *Heaven*, he included this poem because it meant very much to him.

One day the Balys received a letter from a pastor in Massachusetts. For several months the pastor had been visiting a very ill, elderly woman in a hospital. One day the pastor gave her a copy of Mr. Baly's book on heaven, and the woman stayed up all night reading it. The next day she told the pastor that it had brought her great comfort. She died a few days later.

The woman had immigrated from Germany shortly after the war. Her name was Maria Von Wiedermeier; she was Dietrich Bonhoeffer's fiancée at the time of his death. As one writer comments, "From Bonhoeffer to Maria, from Maria to another grieving fiancee, from this fiancee to the parent of the one she loved, from one of his books to other hurting people, then through a friend of his back to Bonhoeffer's Maria as she lay dying in a Boston hospital."[2]

The Impact We Have

I imagine that when we get to heaven we will be astounded at this vast network of care. I am reminded of the classic film *It's a Wonderful Life*. It tells the story of George Bailey, a man who decides to commit suicide after his life falls apart. God sends an angel to rescue him, and the angel shows him what the world would have been like if he had never been born. Once George realizes the effect his seemingly small life has had on everyone in his community, he discovers that it is, indeed, a wonderful life he has been living.

The movie makes a very powerful point: our lives have an effect on those around us far greater than we can see. Each moment, each decision, each act of kindness, will have a ripple effect on the universe. What we do today—or don't do today—will have an impact on someone. This is the way God has designed the world.

George Bailey was given a chance to see what the world would have been like without him. We are not likely to be given that opportunity, which means that we will never know what kind of impact we have had on this world. We may never know the effect of a single encouraging word, of an offer to help someone in trouble, of a prayer lifted up for someone in pain. I suspect when we reach the other side of the veil we will know, and we will be in awe.

God: The Motive to Care Within Us

God has created a world in which we are the ones who care for one another. To put it another way, God cares for us *through* one another. But before God can begin using us to care for one another he does two things: first, God instills in us the desire to care, and second, he provides an example of how to care for one another.

The motive to care for one another comes from the care God has shown us. The apostle John wrote, "Beloved, since

God loved us so much, we also ought to love one another. By this we know that we abide in him and he in us, because he has given us of his Spirit" (1 John 4:11, 13). God's love for us becomes the source of our desire to love one another. We love, says John, because we have been loved *first* (1 John 4:19).

God's love for us, as seen in his acceptance, forgiveness, and care, penetrates our hearts and begins a journey outward to the people around us. If we fail to care for others, we have most likely failed to know that God cares for us. When we grasp the magnitude of God's love for us, we will begin to feel it flow out of our hands and feet and mouths and into the lives of others. God has given us his Spirit, a Spirit of love that will drive us to care for one another.

God: The Example of Care Given for Us

More than just the impetus, God also provides the model by which we care for one another. A Christian is one who is enrolled in the school of charity, and God is the teacher. St. Paul reminded the Christians at Thessalonica, "Now concerning love of the brothers and sisters, you do not need to have anyone write to you, for *you yourselves have been taught by God* to love one another" (1 Thess. 4:9).

God provides for us the *example* of how to care for one another. How does God care for us? God cares for our spiritual life, God cares for the health of our soul, and God provides for our physical needs. God is available, God listens, and God never abandons us. This is how we are to care for one another.

Jesus also left us a clear picture of how to care for one another. He never discouraged people, he spoke the truth in love, and he gave of his time and energy to meet the needs of those around him. He received the poor and the sinful in the same manner as he welcomed the rich and the righteous. He loved all people and wept for their pain. St. Paul told the church in Rome, "Welcome one another, therefore, just *as Christ has welcomed you*" (Rom. 15:7). We are given the model of how we are to treat one another in the example of Jesus.

God: The One Who Cares Through Us

In addition to the motive and the example, God also provides the actual care we give to one another. We are not really caring for one another, but rather, it is God who cares through us. We are merely vessels that carry a great treasure; there is no power within us. The apostle Paul wrote, "But we have this treasure in clay jars, so that it may be made clear that this extraordinary power belongs to God and does not come from us" (2 Cor. 4:7).

There is a story about a little girl who sat by her mother during a church service in which a woman was being baptized. The little girl asked what it was all about, and the mother replied, "Jesus is going to come and wash her sins away and raise her to new life." The little girl replied, "That's good, because I have been coming to this church a long time and I haven't gotten to see him yet."

Where is Jesus? Jesus is alive and well, living in and through those who trust in him and offer themselves as a means by which he can bless others. The best proof of the resurrection of Jesus is the acts of mercy and care that are displayed by those who claim to know him. As the apostle John wrote, "No one has ever seen God; if we love one another, God lives in us, and his love is perfected in us" (1 John 4:12).

God Cures, We Care

Knowing that it is God who cares for others through me has liberated me from the oppressive burden of trying to heal everyone's illnesses, solve everyone's problems, and make everyone whole and happy. We are not the ones who *cure*, we are ones who offer *care*. God is in the business of curing and healing and solving. He has called us to be his hands and feet and mouth, but he has not called us to heal; he has called us to be available.

Pastor and clinical psychologist Kenneth Haugk tells the story of a woman named Ann, whom he had counseled for five years. She had grown tremendously during that time. Just as she was finishing her therapy and was about to part with Dr. Haugk, a crisis occurred in her life that would have normally sent her into an emotional tailspin. Although she experienced sadness, she handled the crisis quite well.

Dr. Haugk was pleased to see that the five years of therapy had made a difference, and that she was now able to handle even the most difficult situations. When he met with her he said, "It looks as if we have done our work well." Ann smiled and said,

> I think it was really God who did it. There were times when I felt so low, so despondent, so out of control that I didn't know what to do. I have an idea that at those times you didn't know what to do with me either. I really believe that God was with me when neither I nor you knew what to do—that God was providing the therapy during those times. . . . We need to give credit where credit is due, and that is with God.[3]

God really does the work of caring through us, but this does not mean that we remain passive. God needs us. That is the way he has chosen to work.

A Biography of Being Cared For

How do we care for one another as God has cared for us? I asked myself this question, and the answer, I found, was right in my own life. I have witnessed God's gracious, loving care through the lives of many different people who have cared for me, as well as through people who have cared for others. They express the many ways we colabor with God in the art of caring for one another.

Just as in caring for ourselves, we care for one another in three ways. We care for physical needs, emotional needs, and spiritual needs. As we care for one another I think it is important that we consider them in this order, though this is the opposite order in which I discussed caring for ourselves. I have noticed that I am more apt to listen to someone give me spiritual guidance if I am certain that they also care for my physical and emotional needs. I do not care how much someone knows until I know how much they care, and I learn how much they care when I see their willingness to give of themselves to meet all of my needs, not just my spiritual ones.

Caring for One Another's Physical Needs

Tony Campolo, a Christian speaker and author, tells of being a guest at a banquet sponsored by a Christian women's organization. During the gathering the president of the organization read an appeal letter from a missionary who needed four thousand dollars for an immediate need. After reading the heart-rending letter, the president said, "I am going to ask our guest speaker, Mr. Campolo, to lead us in prayer that God will meet the need of this dear missionary. Brother Campolo, would you pray?"

"No," said Tony. The president was stunned. "No, I won't pray for God to meet the needs of this missionary. But I'll tell you what I will do. I'll give every dime of cash I have in my pockets and place it on the table. I'm asking each of you to do the same. If we don't have four thousand dollars, I'll pray for God to meet their needs."

"You have a point, Mr. Campolo. We should give sacrificially. We get your point," the president said.

"I am not just trying to make a point," Tony went on. "I challenge you to give what you have now. No credit cards, no checks." He emptied his wallet. Reluctantly, three hundred people emptied their wallets and purses. The amount laid on the table was well over four thousand dollars.

"You see," Tony concluded, "we didn't need to pray that God would provide the resources. They were already there. We had to pray to let them go."

I was stunned when I first heard this story because I realized just how much God has already given us. God has already provided what we need to meet each other's physical needs. All we need to do is let them go.

In addition to meeting the physical needs of one another through our *resources,* we also care for one another by simply being willing to *help.* One morning when my car broke down, I had no way to get it to the repair shop. Dave Castleberry, a good friend, canceled a meeting to help, getting the car to the shop and making sure that it was fixed properly. He was willing to make a sacrifice to help me in a time of need.

If someone is sick, we can help tend to the person or get medical care. If someone is hungry, we can find a way to get food. If someone is lonely, we can make time to come over. If someone is frightened, we can offer a place of safety. In these and many other ways we release the resources God has given us (our money, our time, and our energy) to care for the physical needs of those around us.

Caring for One Another's Souls

Our souls are often in need of care, the kind of care that can only be provided by someone else. Our souls are our emotions and passions, and providing soul care for one another is done through listening, encouraging, and affirming.

Listening

When my soul feels twisted and bent out of shape, I find myself longing for someone to listen to me. I am not talking about a person who merely *hears* my words, but someone who actually *listens* to my heart. A good friend of mine is a trained spiritual director, a person who has learned to listen to the heart. There have been several occasions when I needed someone to help me get in touch with what is really going on inside of me, someone to journey alongside of me as I sift through the emotions and feelings that I am experiencing.

Listening without judgment is a wonderful gift we can give to one another. Without judging, she actively listens and, in doing so, helps me to deal with things I am having trouble understanding. I leave our visits with a feeling of having been heard, and it feels like my soul has been set free.

Encouragement

Not long ago a woman came into my office saying, "You probably don't remember me. Four years ago I was going to leave the ministry, but you listened to me complain, and you helped awaken me to the love of God, and you prayed for me. Ever since then I have stayed in ministry, and in fact, I have grown even deeper in my faith." She had no idea, but the day she said this to me I was feeling very discouraged. Her words lifted me out of my feelings of despair. God once used me to encourage her, and now God was using her to encourage me.

The apostle Paul told his brothers and sisters to "encourage one another" and "build up each other" (see 1 Thess. 4:18; 5:11). We can do that by simply expressing appreciation to the people in our lives. Mark Twain once remarked, "I can live for two months on a good compliment." Encouraging words breathe life into us and energize us. I keep a folder in my file drawer titled, "Encouragement." It is filled with letters and cards and personal notes sent to me over the years. Each time I get a positive note I read it and then put it in the file. When life gets particularly discouraging I pull out the file and peruse these encouraging words.

We need to hear words of encouragement because our world is so full of discouragement. Everywhere around us lurks a reason to lose hope. Caring for one another can mean something as simple as saying, "I believe in you." Words like that breathe life into one's soul.

Spoken Affirmation

In addition to encouragement our souls also need affirmation. To encourage someone is to say, "You can do it!" To affirm someone is to say, "You are valuable." Many times in my life I have been given new life from simple words of affirmation. At one point I was feeling very discouraged about my abilities. I took my mother to listen to a speech given by a person for whom I have great respect. After the evening came to a close this man came up to my mother, who was standing a few feet away from me, and said, "I am awfully proud of your son." He looked over at me and smiled. A feeling of joy overcame me.

Those seven words, seven little words, lifted my soul out of the depths of despair. For the next several days I replayed that sentence in my mind, and each time I was filled with a feeling of exultation. The gifted writer Max Lucado wrote, "Plant a word of love heart-deep in a person's life. Nurture it with a smile and a prayer, and watch what happens."[4] What usually happens is that the person is enabled to walk away refreshed and full of energy. "Good words, " said English poet George Herbert, "are worth much and cost little."[5]

The Power of the Pen

The written word can also be a means of God's grace. The Bible is full of letters written to others as a means of encouragement and affirmation. The simple act of writing a letter to someone may mean the difference between hope and despair. Best-selling author Charles Colson tells the story of Myrtie Howell, "Grandma Howell" as so many knew her, a woman who used her pen to affirm and encourage people in prison.

By the final years of her life, Grandma Howell had lost everyone she loved, and her health was in great decline. She prayed, "Lord, what more can I do for you? If you're ready for me, I'm ready to come. I want to die. Take me." God answered, "Write to prisoners." At first she was afraid. Her writing skills were poor, and she did not know anything about prison ministries. All she knew was that she had been given a job, so she wrote the following letter to the Atlanta Penitentiary. Her grammar may have been wrong, but her heart was right.

> Dear Inmate,
>
> I am a Grandmother who love and care for you who are in a place you had not plans to be. My love and sympathy goes out to you. I am willing to be a friend to you in correspondent. If you like to hear from me, write me. I will answer every letter you write.
>
> A Christian friend,
> Grandmother Howell

The prison chaplain immediately sent her the names of eight inmates and invited her to write to them. Eventually she corresponded with hundreds of inmates, up to forty at a time. As Chuck Colson read the several letters from the stacks she had received he looked at her and said, "Bless you, Myrtie." Myrtie *was* blessed, because she blessed so many. She said, "These last years have been the most fulfilling of my whole life."[6]

My wife has a close friend, Beth Anderson, who is particularly good at this kind of encouragement. I have watched her over the years write notes to many people, telling them how much she believes in them, or how much she sees God doing in their lives. She buoys people's spirits by the simple act of putting a pen to a piece of paper.

Caring for One Another's Spirit

We are also called to care for one another's spiritual needs. Paul prayed for the Ephesians, "I pray that, according to the riches of his glory, he may grant that you may be strengthened *in your inner being* with power through his Spirit" (Eph. 3:16). I believe Paul is referring to our spirits, the part of us that comes to life when we respond to the word of the gospel, the part of us that needs regular renewal through the disciplines of the spiritual life. Two important ways we care for one another's spirits are by proclaiming the message of the gospel and prayer.

Bringing the Word

I first *read* the gospel when I was sixteen years old. The first Bible I ever received was from a friend named Tim. He was a Christian and he prayed that I might become one, too. He was surprised when I asked him if I could borrow one of his Bibles, giving me a used copy of the Living Bible. "Where should I start reading?" I asked. "This is a big book!" We were both pretty young, and we were not biblically trained, but he did tell me that the Book of Acts and the Psalms were pretty interesting. I read passages from the Bible each night before falling asleep. The words were like seeds being planted in my spirit.

I first *heard* the gospel from a man named Pat. He was a part-time fireman and sometime street evangelist who wore beach clothes and carried a tattered Bible. I came to him with searching and difficult questions about God when I was seventeen years old, and he took me seriously. He helped me read the Bible and understand it, and eventually he presented the basic message of the gospel to me. A few days later I asked God—if he was real—to start working in my life. God has, and has never stopped.

Tim and Pat were caring for my spirit. Others would come along in my life and become my teachers and guides along the way. God has chosen to put his truths in the mouths of men and women. Our spirits are made alive through words spoken by other human beings. Each of us has the opportunity to become a "living epistle": "You are *a letter of Christ,* prepared by us, written not with ink but with the Spirit of the living God, not on tablets of stone but on tablets of human hearts" (2 Cor. 3:3).

Prayer

"There is no greater intimacy with another than that which is built through holding him or her up in prayer," writes the Quaker author Douglas V. Steere.[7] He goes on to tell the story of John Frederic Oberlin, a pastor who devoted an hour each morning to prayer for his individual parishioners. Steere notes, "We are told that as they went past his house at this hour in the morning, they did so in quiet, for they knew what was happening there."

We live in a universe with a God who is everywhere, and simply by talking to this God things change. Prayer makes things happen. If this is true, then one of the greatest things we can do for one another is to pray. In prayer we are not trying to change God's mind, or coax God into doing something he does not want to do, but rather, we are cooperating with God's active love.

It never ceases to amaze me when I find out someone has been doing so. I covet all of those prayers. I could not imagine what my life would be like without them. What I sometimes call miracles in my life are probably answers to someone's prayers for me.

I know a man who goes to his church and prays every morning between six and seven o'clock. During that time he does nothing but pray for others. One day he sent me a note saying that he had been led to pray for me, and after a week of interceding on my behalf, thought he heard the angels sigh, saying, "He's alright." The note mentioned the date of the week he had prayed. I looked back at my calendar and realized that his prayers had come during a trying time in my life. I am certain that his prayers made a difference.

Too Short Not to Give What We Can

The following is another "Life is too short . . . " list, only this list involves ways we have opportunities to care for one another.

Life is too short to refuse to offer a kind word to someone who needs it, too short to turn a deaf ear to someone who is hurting, and too short to pass by someone who needs a hand. Life is too short to withhold a Word of life, too short not to pray for someone we know is in trouble, and too short to neglect that note of encouragement we were meaning to send.

Life is too short not to send toys to children with life-threatening diseases, too short not to offer to babysit for exhausted parents, and too short not to give your co-worker a bouquet of flowers. Life is too short not to shovel your neighbor's walk, too short not to visit a retirement home for an afternoon, and too short not to spend a morning writing letters to people we love. Life is too short to let a week pass without hearing someone say, "Thank you. You really didn't have to . . . "

Even though our random acts of kindness may seem small, each thing we do for one another has a cosmic significance. As Herman Melville pointed out, "A thousand fibers connect us with our fellow men; and among those fibers, as sympathetic threads, our actions run as causes, and they come back to us as effects."

The Quality of Mercy Is Not Strained

St. Francis de Sales believed that each time we perform an act of charity "God immediately gives an increase in charity."[8] When we care for others, our capacity to care is increased. As this capacity increases, *we* benefit as well. We will find that both giver and receiver are blessed, and in the giving there is no strain. As William Shakespeare wrote,

> The quality of mercy is not strain'd;
> it droppeth as the gentle rain from heaven
> Upon the place beneath: it is twice bless'd;
> it blesseth him that gives and him that takes.[9]

Epilogue

The love in which God made us never had a beginning.
In it we have our beginning.

JULIAN OF NORWICH

After reading this book you may still be struggling with God's acceptance, God's forgiveness, and God's care. If so, there is no need to despair. Reading a book may be the beginning of the journey. Or perhaps it is yet another voice whispering the same ideas you have been learning, another witness to the truths that are becoming more and more a part of you.

My own story is one of continued learning. I have certainly not finished my journey, and in many ways I have only begun. Each day promises another chance to lean into God's love. There are days in which I wonder if I have really come to accept my acceptance, times when I doubt my complete forgiveness, and moments when I question God's providential care. Then suddenly I find myself in a difficult situation and notice that I am more at liberty to trust than to question God. It is then that I realize that the promises are taking hold of me and shaping who I am.

We do not have to comprehend God's love to appreciate it or to live gratefully within it. As we grow in this gratitude we will find ourselves increasingly able to risk loving ourselves and one another. Our longing for *perfection* will be replaced by a desire for *progress;* we will substitute the making of resolutions (which are all about willpower and achievement and success) with prayer; we will cease berating ourselves for our weaknesses and begin befriending our imperfections; our brokenness will no longer frighten us but instead become an occasion for grace.

There is a story—perhaps only a legend—about the apostle John that stays with me. It is said that in the evening of his long life he would often sit and teach young disciples about all that Jesus said and did for hours at a time. One day one of the disciples complained, "John, you always talk about love, about God's love for us and about our love for one another. Why don't you tell us about something else besides love?" John, the disciple who once laid his head upon the heart of Jesus, is said to have replied, "Because there is nothing else, just love . . . love . . . love."[1]

There are many teachings that will capture our attention, new ideas that will rush to our minds, but none more important than the love of God, shed abroad in our heart, spilling out to everyone who happens to bump into us. God's love, as Julian of Norwich noted, never had a beginning, but in it we have our beginning.

May God bless you as you begin walking along the path of love, and may God's promise to love you fill your heart, soul, and mind, and may it give you strength. I share the certainty of St. Paul who wrote, "I am confident of this, that the one who began a good work among you will bring it to completion by the day of Jesus Christ" (Phil. 1:6).

Notes

Introduction

1. In order to highlight important words or ideas, I have added italics to many of the quotes in this book. As here, please be aware that the italics are mine and not part of the original work.

2. James Hillman and Michael Ventura, *We've Had a Hundred Years of Psychotherapy—and the World's Getting Worse* (San Francisco: HarperSanFrancisco, 1992).

3. Evelyn Underhill, *An Anthology of the Love of God* (Wilton, CT: Morehouse Barlow, 1976), 15.

4. G. K. Chesterton, *Orthodoxy* (New York: Doubleday, 1990), 11.

Part I: Knowing God's Acceptance

Chapter 1: God's Acceptance

1. Peter van Breeman, *As Bread that Is Broken* (Denville, NJ: Dimension, 1974), 14.

2. Richard J. Foster and James Bryan Smith, *Devotional Classics* (San Francisco: HarperSanFrancisco, 1993), 107.

3. Evelyn Underhill, *An Anthology of the Love of God*, 45.

4. G. K. Chesterton, *Orthodoxy*, 52.

5. Evelyn Underhill, *An Anthology of the Love of God*, 47.

6. Brennan Manning, *The Ragamuffin Gospel* (Sisters, OR: Multnomah, 1990), 214.

7. Alfred, Lord Tennyson, *In Memorium,* in *The Oxford Anthology of English Literature*, vol. 3 (Oxford Univ. Press, 1975), 865.

8. Frederick Buechner, *Wishful Thinking* (San Francisco: HarperSanFrancisco, 1973), 91.

9. St. Francis de Sales, *On the Love of God*, vol. 1 (Rockford, IL: Tan Books, 1974), 193.

10. Louis Bouyer, ed., *A History of Christian Spirituality*, vol. 3 (New York: Seabury, 1982), 100.

11. Gerard Manley Hopkins, "The Blessed Virgin Compared to the Air We Breathe," in *Poems of Gerard Manley Hopkins* (Mt. Vernon, NY: Peter Pauper, 1955), 51.

12. I first heard this statement from Brennan Manning. He uses it frequently, and it has helped many people grasp God's love because of its simplicity and truth.

13. Donald McCullough, *Waking from the American Dream* (Downers Grove, IL: InterVarsity, 1988), 122.

14. Evelyn Underhill, *An Anthology of the Love of God*, 44.

15. These words are a compilation of Henri Nouwen, Brennan Manning, and my own.

16. Frederick Buechner, *The Magnificent Defeat* (New York: Seabury, 1983), 35.

17. The original source of this quote is unknown to me. I first read it in Brennan Manning, *The Ragamuffin Gospel*, 34.

18. Joseph Oppitz, C.SS.R., ed., *Alphonsus Liguori—The Redeeming Love of Christ* (New York: New York City Press, 1992), 7.

Chapter 2: Accepting Ourselves

1. John Powell, *Why Am I Afraid to Tell You Who I Am?* (Allen, TX: Argus Communications, 1969), 13.

2. Peter van Breeman, *As Bread that Is Broken,* 15.

3. G. K. Chesterton, *Orthodoxy,* 15.

4. C. S. Lewis, *As the Ruin Falls,* in *Poems,* ed. Walter Hooper (New York: Harcourt Brace Jovanovich, 1977), 109.

5. T. S. Eliot, *The Cocktail Party,* in *The Complete Poems and Plays* (New York: Harcourt Brace Jovanovich, 1971), 308, 348.

6. St. Francis de Sales, *On the Love of God,* vol. 1, 130–31.

7. Evelyn Underhill, *The Spiritual Life* (Wilton, CT: Morehouse Barlow, 1955), 67–68.

8. Dietrich Bonhoeffer, *Life Together* (San Francisco: HarperSanFrancisco, 1976), 110–11.

9. This distinction comes from Evelyn Underhill, *An Anthology of the Love of God,* 188.

10. Brennan Manning, *The Ragamuffin Gospel,* 152.

11. John Powell, *Why Am I Afraid to Love?* (Allen, TX: Argus Communications, 1972), 22.

12. G. K. Chesterton, *Orthodoxy,* 120.

13. See Henri Nouwen, *Life of the Beloved* (New York: Crossroads, 1992), 28.

Chapter 3: Accepting One Another

1. John Powell, *Why Am I Afraid to Love?,* 24.

2. Peter van Breeman, *As Bread that Is Broken,* 126–27.

3. Thomas Merton, *No Man Is an Island* (New York: Harcourt Brace Jovanovich, 1983), 176.

4. Frederick Buechner, *The Magnificent Defeat,* 42.

5. Evelyn Underhill, *An Anthology of the Love of God,* 212–213.

6. Thomas Merton, *No Man Is an Island,* 7–8.

7. St. Augustine, *Confessions,* bk. 10, ch. 4 (New York: Penguin, 1984), 209.

Part II: Receiving God's Forgiveness

Chapter 4: God's Forgiveness

1. Peter van Breeman, *As Bread that Is Broken,* 59.

2. Brennan Manning, *The Ragamuffin Gospel,* 28.

3. Richard J. Foster, *Celebration of Discipline* (San Francisco: Harper-SanFrancisco, 1988), 143.

4. Wesley wrote this in his journal on May 24, 1738. *The Works of John Wesley,* vol. 18, *Journals and Diaries,* ed. Ward & Hetzenrater (Nashville: Abingdon, 1988), 249–250.

5. Charles Stanley, *The Gift of Forgiveness* (Nashville: Thomas Nelson, 1991), 95.

6. Evelyn Underhill, *An Anthology of the Love of God,* 187.

Chapter 5: Forgiving Ourselves

1. Lewis Smedes, *Forgive & Forget* (New York: Pocket Books, 1984), 99.

2. Charles Stanley, *The Gift of Forgiveness,* 147.

3. Foster and Smith, *Devotional Classics,* 101.

4. Robert van de Weyer, ed., *Selected Readings from Kierkegaard,* Spiritual Classics Series (New York: Fleming H. Revell, 1991), 62.

5. The phrase "redemptive remembering" comes from Lewis Smedes, *Forgive & Forget,* 173.

6. Lewis Smedes, *Forgive & Forget,* 99.

Chapter 6: Forgiving One Another

1. C. S. Lewis, *The Joyful Christian* (New York: Macmillan, 1977), 141.

2. G. K. Chesterton, *Orthodoxy,* 95

3. Lewis Smedes, *Forgive & Forget,* 170.

4. I am indebted to Charles Stanley's book *The Gift of Forgiveness* for helping me discover these important aspects of forgiving one another.

Part III: Experiencing God's Love

Chapter 7: God's Care

1. George Muller, *Autobiography* (Grand Rapids, MI: Baker, 1981), 110.

2. Rev. G. B. F. Hallock, *2500 Best Modern Illustrations* (New York: Harper & Brothers, 1935), 289.

3. The original source is unknown to me. I quote it from Ron DelBene, *When I'm Alone* (Nashville: Upper Room, 1988), 23–24.

4. George Muller, *Autobiography,* 110.

5. *The Works of St. Patrick* from *Ancient Christian Writers: The Words of the Fathers in Translation,* trans. and ann. L. Bieher (New York: Newman, 1953), 71.

6. Foster and Smith, *Devotional Classics,* 101.

Chapter 8: Caring for Ourselves

1. This is the answer to the opening question of the Westminster Cathechism.

2. Thomas Moore, *Care of the Soul* (New York: HarperCollins, 1992), xi. I am indebted to Tim and Lori Gillach for introducing me to this book exactly when I needed it.

3. Thomas Moore, *Care of the Soul,* 14.

4. See Dallas Willard, *The Spirit of the Disciplines* (San Francisco: HarperSanFrancisco, 1988), 77.

5. C. S. Lewis, *The Screwtape Letters* (New York: Macmillan, 1962), 20.

6. Robert van de Weyer, *The Way of Holiness* (London: Fount, 1992), 25.

7. Johann Arndt, *True Christianity* (New York: Paulist, 1979), 98.

8. Marva J. Dawn, *Keeping the Sabbath Wholly* (Grand Rapids, MI: Eerdmans, 1989), 4.

9. T. S. Eliot, *Four Quartets,* in *The Complete Poems and Plays,* 121.

10. Richard J. Foster, *Prayer: Finding the Heart's True Home* (San Francisco: HarperSanFrancisco, 1992).

11. Richard J. Foster, *Celebration of Discipline,* 63.

12. I would recommend all of their writings to any who would desire to try this exercise. New Reader's Press has undertaken the task of republishing some of Laubach's works in *The Heritage Collection* (Syracuse, NY, 1990); Brother Lawrence, *The Practice of the Presence of God,* trans. John J. Delaney (New York: Doubelday, 1977); Thomas Kelley, *A Testament of Devotion* (San Francisco: HarperSanFrancisco, 1992); Jean-Pierre de Caussade, *The Sacrament of the Present Moment,* trans. Kitty Muggeridge (San Francisco: Harper & Row, 1982).

13. Doris Longacre preached a sermon containing some of these "life is too short" ideas in 1978. When she died a year later they were read at her memorial service.

14. *Men's Health* (March 1994): 17.

15. Thomas Moore, *Care of the Soul,* 95.

Chapter 9: Caring for One Another

1. Dietrich Bonhoeffer, *Cost of Discipleship* (New York: Macmillan, 1975), p. 20. Poem translated by Geoffrey Winthrop Young.

2. This quote, as well as the story, is taken from David Jeremiah, *Acts of Love* (Gresham, OR: Vision House, 1994), 36–38.

3. Kenneth G. Haugk, *Christian Caregiving* (Minneapolis, MN: Augsburg, 1984), 29.

4. David Jeremiah, *Acts of Love,* 62.

5. George Herbert, quoted in David Jeremiah, *Acts of Love,* 186.

6. This story is told in Charles Colson, *Loving God* (New York: Harper Paperbacks, 1987), 267–76.

7. Foster and Smith, *Devotional Classics,* 88–89.

8. St. Francis de Sales, *On the Love of God,* vol. 1, p. 165.

9. William Shakespeare, *The Merchant of Venice,* IV, i., in *The Complete Works of William Shakespeare,* vol. 1 (Roslyn, NY: Walter J. Black, 1937), 243.

Epilogue

1. John Powell, *Why Am I Afraid to Love?,* 119–20.

Scripture Index

Index of Names